START YOUR OWN DAMN CULT

A Founder's Field Guide

By: Gagan J Levy

Edited By   Marguerite Hofmeyr (sentiency.co)
Designed By   Baha Fenerci (driftroot.com)
Powered By   Guru (weareguru.com)
Published By   Puhpowee (gotppw.com)

Dedications

I feel my late little brother Gavin "Metta G's" hands on my hands now as I write this. Even after all the good that he did in this world leading the amazing hunger relief nonprofit Conscious Alliance, my brother felt that he hadn't found his true purpose. He wanted me to help him find it, just as soon as he got better. I didn't get that chance. In May of 2018, my brother left his body, this world, and a lot of people that loved him dearly. My bond with Gavin may truly be where the phrase "love you like a brother" comes from. As much as he looked up to his big brother, he is the one who led me towards a path of selfless service, opened my eyes to the joy of giving back and was truly the inspiration for me to move from business as usual to business as service.

I do this work to increase joy and reduce suffering and bring about a world that may be more regenerative, compassionate and thriving for my daughters and primary teachers, Jaya Grace and Metta Jade to inherit. You are the loves of my life and teach me how to be a better father, man, leader and human every day.

And so I offer a guiding Metta "Loving Kindness" prayer for our life and work together. Shared with me by Buddhist Meditation teacher Sharon Salzberg, inscribed on my brother's Gavin tombstone and carried forth in the name of my daughter.

May All Be Peaceful

May All Be Happy

May All Be Well

May All Be Safe

May All Be Free From Suffering

Foreword by Haider Nazar

Every founder has been handed the same playbooks. They teach us how to find product-market fit, raise capital, acquire customers, and scale. But almost none of them teach us how to build something people would follow to the ends of the earth. That is what this book does.

Because the next generation of great companies will not be built on clever models or perfect unit economics. They will be built on belief and led by founders who know how to create energy, not just value. Founders that create movements, not markets.

Gagan Levy understands that better than anyone I know. I've had the privilege of building alongside him for years as a partner, co-founder, and friend. He is fearless, spiritual, playful, and radically inclusive. Gagan doesn't just talk about community; he lives it through consistency, compassion, and conviction.

His apprenticeship with the great wisdom keeper Ram Dass isn't something he keeps tucked away in a meditation practice. It shows up in how he leads, how he listens, and how he makes people feel seen. Whether in a boardroom or a brainstorm, he treats leadership as an act of love. And the wild thing is, it works.

When you lead with love, you attract people who want to belong, not just transact. When you lead with purpose, you create alignment no marketing budget can buy. The same qualities that make you a better human (awareness, empathy, fearlessness) also make you a better founder.

One moment stands out very clearly. An investor was ready to back us and the capital, which we desperately needed, would have helped us move faster. But Gagan asked a simple question: "What is the energy of this capital?" We passed. It wasn't easy, but it was right. That decision preserved the integrity of what we were building and reinforced a truth I now carry with me: money has intention, and how you bring it in shapes what you build.

That is exactly what Start Your Own Damn Cult is about. This is not another how-to-scale book. It's a field guide for founders who want to build something magnetic, alive, and aligned. Not a cult in the usual sense, but the kind of company that inspires loyalty beyond transactions. Most founders chase growth. The great ones create gravity.

This book makes that kind of leadership accessible. It shows how devotion is earned through meaning, not manipulation. How authenticity is not just a personal trait, but a business strategy. How love and discipline, spirituality and scale, can coexist.

If you're holding this book, you already feel the tension between growth and meaning. So read with an open heart. Let this book challenge how you think about leadership and belonging. Because cults aren't built through persuasion. They're built through connection. And that is what Gagan Levy teaches best.

About the Foreword Author

Haider Nazar is the co-founder and CEO of Maha Global, an AI powered decision intelligence platform focused on helping organizations realize their true value by aligning belief, reputation, and performance. A five-time founder with multiple exits and trusted advisor to leaders across sectors, he has worked with organizations including Amgen, Honda, Medtronic, Target, and Vertex. As Gagan Levy's cofounder and partner in Maha Global, Haider shares a core conviction: that business can be a force for good—and that what separates movements from companies is belief, and the courage to act on it.

Table of Contents

A Note on Appropriation
(aka how not to be a jackass with sacred stuff)

Before we dance too far down this wild, wonderful path, I want to pause here, in the doorway, and offer a bow. The architecture behind this book, the eight limbs of yoga, is absolutely not mine. It is an ancient framework, rooted in the spiritual traditions of India, first articulated in the Yoga Sutras of Patanjali over two thousand years ago. This ancient system was born long before I was scribbling manifestos in a Moleskine or naming a creative agency - guru after spiritual guides. These teachings were not meant to sell products or optimize the founder's flow. They were/are practices of liberation, devotion, and deep inner alignment.

In drawing from this well, I do so with humility and am not here to rebrand the sacred, but rather to sit beside it. To listen closely. I've done my best to adapt this path with reverence and curiosity, and to translate these limbs in a way that feels alive in the context I know best: building something meaningful (often organizations or movements), with others. Doing this from the inside out and carrying this philosophy into new rooms, in new language, for new ears.

While naming my debt, I offer this adaptation as an imperfect bridge always in conversation with the roots it rises from. Know that I am doing my best and centering my intention to stay in right relationship with the wisdom, with the world, and with each other. My experience is that this body of insight can grow leaders who are freer, truer, and more aligned and offer a path towards liberated leadership.

And to Ram Dass: teacher, trickster, mirror, map. Your life was a transmission of truth wrapped in mischief and kindness. Your presence made the sacred accessible without ever diluting its depth. You walked the line between East and West with barefoot grace, and left a trail for the rest of us to stumble along, laughing and crying as we go. I was lucky enough to be in your "Soul Pod," sitting at your feet learning from you firsthand and verklempt as you sing "row row row your boat…life is but a dream" to my daughter swimming around you in the ocean.

I am absolutely honored to carry your legacy forward as a board member of the foundation that bears your name. This book is steeped in your wisdom, even when it's not quoting you outright.

Thank you for reminding us:

We're all just walking each other home.

- Ram Dass

INTRO

"The spiritual journey is individual, and highly personal. It can't be organized or regulated. It isn't true that everyone should follow one path. Listen to your own truth."

— **Ram Dass**

"A sense of humor… is superior to any religion so far devised"

— **Tom Robbins**

Welcome to the Founder's Field Guide

Conscious entrepreneurs, future business mystics, purpose pioneers, intrepid intrapreneurs and wandering children of the light step right up, step right up! Bring all of you: your proud accomplishments, your polished pitch deck and your messy morning pages, your investor inventory and your inner child, your parent's expectations and your partner's desires, the meditation method you talk about more than you practice, your company mission statement that still needs "something more," and the aspirational "you" that you know is possible. Grab a fair trade, gluten-free, non-GMO, regenerative organic certified s'more and sit your firefly-lit face by Brother Gagan's bonfire.

This is a book for the misfits with a mission. For the ones who feel the pull to **build something sacred, not just scalable.** Those who know that the best business insights might come from a psychedelic trip, a Maya Angelou poem, or a surf at sunrise. No ceremony required. No secret handshake. No guru but the one staring back at you from the mirror.

The mirror that met me on top of the Mayacamas Mountains, overlooking the volcanic caldera of Saint Helena in Northern California, didn't hold a guru or a ghost. What I saw was someone mid-tide, catching his breath between who he'd been and who he was becoming. I'd taken an intentional dose of psilocybin mushrooms to loosen the grip of my everyday mind and let something deeper surface.

I didn't want to escape or transcend, just to clear space, to listen, to write, and to remember. My brother Gavin, the closest human to my soul in this lifetime, had passed a year earlier and I'd just finished yoga teacher training. My heart was cracked open and my inbox was, for once, quiet.

What I found up there was an unexpected, yet obvious opportunity. The only way to move in a direction I actually gave a damn about was to find a framework, filter and practice to integrate everything I'd collected along the way the chaos, the lessons, the unofficial MBA I earned through serial entrepreneurship, and all the sideways wisdom that life hands you when you're paying attention. Once I started weaving those threads, things stopped feeling so scattered. I stopped building from panic and started building from coherence and soul. The concept of work / life balance simplified to just life balance.

Harvard Business Review once published a piece on what really motivates people, emotionally, mentally and even spiritually at work. Turns out, the magic sauce is something called *the progress principle* and that the biggest emotional and motivational boost we get during our day, quarter or even career comes from making progress on something that actually matters. **Meaningful movement.**

And yeah, we all need that hit in different doses, but the bottom line is that we want to feel like we're going somewhere and not just rearranging deck chairs on the capitalist cruise ship.

So maybe it was the mushrooms or maybe it was just grief alchemizing into clarity, but I decided to run a little thought experiment: **what if the same eight limbs of yoga that has helped me heal and grow as a human...could actually help me become a better leader...and build a better business.**

Because business doesn't need to be soulless to succeed and the soul doesn't need to be sacrificed at the altar of scale. I wrote this because the world is brimming with bright minds and brave hearts stuck in outdated models.

They celebrate growth but forget to ask: what for? This book exists for the ones who are done with that. Let's be honest, "business as usual" is a dying myth. But something more beautiful is already rising quietly and bravely crafted by those willing to build from a different center. Swapping the jargon for joy. Keeping the strategy, but combining it with soul.

If you're here, chances are you've climbed to the "false mountaintop" already, the one made of gold stars and semi-hollow victories.

Maybe you're wildly "successful," but something deeper is whispering that there's more. This book is here to tell you that you're not delusional. You're waking up to purpose and to that strange inner certainty that says: this life wants something more from me than quarterly goals and a clean inbox.

or shouting

This book is a step-by-step founder's field guide for that awakening into liberated leadership. Audacious enough to challenge the system, clear enough to change it, created with equal parts bold imagination and unflinching moral clarity. Big vision, steady spine.

Business badass who meditates at dawn? Punk strategist rewriting the rules by night? This is for the mother building an empire between school runs - done apologizing, done explaining, done pretending she's not the most powerful one in the room.

A blueprint for building your own conscious cult shaped by devotion, animated by coherence, and driven by a fierce brand-love that doesn't blink, flinch, or wait for permission.

Part myth, part mythology, with smudges and margin notes. Words crossed out and rewritten like it's been on retreat with you. Or road-tripped across the country in a dust-laced van following the Grateful Dead, pages dog-eared, lyrics in the margins, incense in the spine.

I want you to use this book like you'd use an old vinyl. Drop the needle on it, hear it crackle to life and let it play. Tango with it if you like tension and jitterbug if you're feeling wild, just don't sit this one out. **Lean in and then remember how to build the thing only you can build.** This isn't a shortcut or a hack, but a compass and an evolving hand-scrawled map for those ready to remember what really matters.

⚡ Cult: The Word, the Myth, the Movement

What a word, right? ***Cult.*** It's hard to say it without feeling something: a little unease, a flicker of curiosity and maybe even a jolt of recognition or a ping of disgust.

It's been dragged through the mud, co-opted, weaponized and reduced to a stigmatized warning label. But look closer, and the root is surprisingly tender: *cultus* - to care, to inhabit devotion, to make meaning through attention. That's what we're really talking about. Forget obedience and delusion. This is about devotion.

Cult is just culture with fewer syllables. The only difference is time. A cult is culture in its rawest form: still malleable, still alive, still charged with the wildness of its origin. And we're here to build **culture with soul…**with many souls with many cults.

So let's start with the real question: how do you build something so alive, so dialed-in to your particular flavor of madness, that people start whispering about it in corners and following you down unlit hallways just to see what happens next? That's what we call "cult energy" and yes, it starts with you.

You're not here to copy-paste someone else's success map. You're here to tune your own signal until it sings. You're here to build something that pulses, buzzes, growls if it needs to. It's like slipping into your favorite fever dream and finding out that the band's already playing your song.

This kind of clarity doesn't arrive in a Google Doc but crawls up your spine when you least expect it and builds from the unshakable, unmarketable parts of you, the ones that still get goosebumps when something feels right, even if it doesn't make sense in a spreadsheet.

Before you build your movement, you have to start with the unique clarity and excitement that lives inside your own bones. If that part's scattered, the rest is just performance art in ergonomic chairs. So we begin here. In the guts. In the static and the tremble and the frequency that only you can hear when the world goes quiet. You just need to remember where your fire lives. You need to walk back to the origin point, barefoot and messy. *possibly with glitter*

The first cult is you. Start there. Everything else will follow.

Confessions of a Cult Catalyzer

Let's get one thing straight from the start: I love building cults.

Not the robe-wearing, Kool-Aid-chugging kind. No isolated compounds, no creepy charismatics. I'm talking about the good kind of cult: the kind that heals, that sparks joy, that magnetizes people into a shared vibe of belonging and momentum.

unless you count your inner child

Call it what you want: a family, tribe, movement, conscious brand, purpose-driven organization, but ultimately you're here to build something worth believing in.

Something that hits deeper than metrics and shinier than a pitch deck. You want resonance, you want to find your people, and you want your work to matter.

and sometimes lost myself

Over the past two decades, I've found myself inside the engine rooms of some of the most alive movements of our time: socially responsible business, impact investing, regenerative agriculture, the destigmatization of psychedelics, consciousness through media, and yes, even a little campaign called Obama '08. Guru, the creative agency I founded, has often stumbled into being the invisible amplifier behind the signal, helping purpose-driven people start and scale the cults that changed culture.

Eventually, I noticed a pattern. A type of code. A secret sauce, if you will, though it tastes a lot like coconut oil and righteous rebellion. The best movements weren't born from slick branding or VC-fueled blitzscaling, but emerged from the soul. From a founder waking up to their purpose, like our client Yvonne Chouinard from Patagonia proudly proclaiming, **"Let My People Go Surfing"** and having the courage to live it out loud. From a small ripple that caught the right wind and became a wave.

or audacity

What This Is Not

This book is not a permission slip to centralize power, override consent, or confuse devotion with obedience. If at any point this work asks you to abandon your agency, outsource your discernment, or elevate a leader above the work itself, you've taken a wrong turn.

Healthy cults dissolve dependency. They increase sovereignty, not submission. They train people to listen more deeply to themselves, not to me or any other founder.

Founded From The Inside Out

Before we dive into the ancient scaffolding that's about to blow the roof off your business plan, we have to go somewhere even deeper: YOU. Before you tell the world who you are, make sure you've asked yourself.

the good kind

Because every great cult starts with a compelling frequency. And that frequency? It starts with you, the founder, the beautiful, chaotic, over-caffeinated human who got hit with a vision and decided to do something absurdly brave...build something real.

See, this work moves in waves. And the first wave? It's not branding or product-market fit. It's also not a catchy name or a half-baked biz plan. **It's the crystallization of the soul of your business or cult or movement or whatever you want to call it.** It's the part where you stop performing, get quiet, and remember why the hell you care in the first place. You trace the signal, that raw, unfiltered frequency of you, and you sit with it long enough for it to start making sense again. This is the moment you catch your purpose by the tail and whisper, "Alright, let's do this." With clarity of purpose and a commitment to utilize it as a filter for this business and for all future endeavors - you will pull yourself out of the trap set by a society gone mad.

That soul-truth is what we build around, because once you have it, everything else starts to click. The team finds its rhythm and the brand starts to hum. The energy gets sticky in the best way, not from hustle or hype, but from coherence. From alignment and from the sweet spot where who you are and what you're building finally high-five each other.

So let's start there with the first pulse, the root of the root and the soul of your business and catalyze a movement from the inside out.

Reflection:

The best way to remember who you really are is to look into your dreams and desires for this world and work backwards.

This isn't about locking in your life's mission. It's about listening.

What is something — a cause, a problem, a way of serving — that you could imagine devoting real energy to right now? Why does it matter to you?

Trust that this answer can change. What matters is beginning the conversation.

....

....

....

....

....

....

....

....

....

Practice: The "Future You" Documentary

Ten minute guided meditation: Imagine a documentary crew is profiling your company 10 years from now. What story are you telling? What are you doing? What are the words used to describe it? What is the change you set out to create? What have you accomplished? What is the impact you've had on the world? Who have been the beneficiaries (the people positively affected) of your hard work? What do you want to be remembered for?

A PATH TO LIBERATED LEADERSHIP

Up to this point, we've been circling the why.

We've been clearing ground, naming myths, and locating the deeper motivation behind the work you feel called to do. That's intentional. Because before you can talk about leadership, you have to talk about orientation. About what kind of life and work you're actually trying to build.

What comes next is different.

This is where we shift from context to practice.

From philosophy to formation.

From naming the calling to developing the capacity to carry it.

What follows in this book is not a grab bag of ideas or a greatest-hits list of founder wisdom. And it's also not a straight line, a ladder, or a checklist you graduate from once and for all.

It's a leadership learning landscape — a set of inner and outer capacities that strong, resilient, human-centered leaders learn to access, embody, and move between over time. Think less "progression" and more orientation. Less staircase, more compass.

Before we cannonball in, I want to lay down a pathway that didn't fully reveal itself until I started teaching this framework out loud, in rooms, in workshops, in founder circles, in all those places where leadership isn't theoretical but lived, messy, embodied. What I noticed was that the thing people clung to most wasn't the underlying philosophy (at least not at first), it was the **leadership capacities** hidden inside the Codes.

Some founders walked out of a session saying, "Ah, okay. I finally see where I actually am as a leader" or "Now I know what I'm practicing toward" or even some whispering, "Shit… I've got work to do."

The Leadership Learning Path became a kind of compass—a way to locate yourself inside your own evolution and a living map for how you grow. Leadership is often treated as something you either "have" or don't. As if confidence, clarity, and steadiness just arrive with a title, a funding round, or a bigger team. In fact, leadership is the slow-burning, sometimes sweaty, often uncomfortable, occasionally ecstatic work of becoming someone your vision and people can rely on.

And every Code in this book comes with a leadership identity, a wayfinding tool that you will learn to embody in that code. Not an identity in the branding sense, but an identity in the capacity sense. A new way of relating to yourself, to your team, to your purpose, to your energy, and to the world.

This is the developmental, sequential spine beneath the codes. And with all leadership development....it's basically therapy with better vocabulary. This path doesn't rank leaders as better or worse. It simply names **different kinds of readiness**. Different ways of relating to responsibility, power, attention, and trust.

Most leadership training is built backwards: it offers tools before orientation, scripts before soul, and management tricks before teaching you how to stay regulated enough to not set yourself on fire.

We flip that by helping you to understand:

- what kind of leadership is being asked of you now;
- the inner wiring you need and nervous system upgrades required;
- -and what capacities you're actively developing and what comes next, without rushing it

Eight Leadership Capacities To Cultivate

Below is the leadership arc this book will guide you through. Read it not as a test, but as an orientation. A sense of what you'll be learning to practice as we move forward.

1. Foundational Leadership

This is where leadership begins: with integrity.

Foundational leadership is about building trust through accountability. It's the capacity to lead from values rather than impulse, and to create coherence between intention and action. Without this foundation, everything else becomes fragile and no amount of vision can save a wobbly moral spine.

Can you be trusted with responsibility?

....

2. Reflective Leadership

Here, leadership turns inward.

Reflective leaders develop the ability to see themselves clearly: their habits, blind spots, and default reactions. This awareness creates choice and instead of repeating patterns unconsciously, you begin to lead with intention. Polish the mirror, love yourself and skip the soft lighting.

Can you learn from yourself in real time?

....

3. Grounded Leadership

This is about presence.

It's the calm, confident capacity to take your comfortable seat without posturing or performance. Your leadership stabilizes the room. People feel clearer around you. You can stop borrowing someone else's CEO voice now.

Can others feel where you stand?

....

4. Regulated Leadership

Leadership becomes inseparable from nervous system awareness.

Regulated leaders can hold pressure without exporting it. They respond rather than react. Their steadiness creates psychological safety and operational clarity. This is where caffeine meets its match.

Can you stay resourced under stress?

....

5. Discerning Leadership

Discerning leadership is about the capacity for wisdom and insight.

It's the ability to listen beneath the noise, to create space for insight, and to recognize what actually needs attention. Silence becomes productive rather than uncomfortable.

Can you hear what matters most?

....

6. Focused Leadership

Focused leadership brings precision.

Attention becomes a tool rather than a liability. Priorities clarify, energy consolidates and progress compounds. This is where shiny objects go to die.

Can you protect what matters from distraction?

....

7. Embodied Leadership

Embodied leadership is integration.

This is where leadership stops being something you manage and starts being something you emanate. You embody a flow state where values show up in behavior and presence becomes consistent. When this clicks, you'll stop (whoa)man-splaining so much.

Can you live what you lead?

....

8. Liberated Leadership

Finally, leadership releases.

Liberated leaders build systems, cultures, and movements that don't depend on constant control. The work carries itself forward. Leadership becomes shared and your ego gets a gold watch and gentle escort out.

Can the work move without you at the center?

....

Before We Begin

This work was never meant to be done in isolation. Leadership without reflection, without peers, and without feedback loops tends to drift. Use this with people who will tell you the truth.

You don't need to be anywhere on this path yet. You don't need to diagnose yourself or jump ahead. This is simply the terrain we're about to walk.

In the next section, I'll introduce the deeper structure that holds this leadership path together—the underlying framework that gives it coherence and durability. From there, we'll step into the practices themselves, one code at a time.

For now, let this be an orientation, a breath before the descent and a look at the trail before we take the first step.

Sacred Secret Sauce

So you can smell something tasty wafting in from the kitchen and you want to know the recipe for bubula's business bouillabaisse, do ya? Okay, you paid for your ticket, you're tall enough to get on the ride, so away we go. Long ago, before calendars and capitalism, before people mistook productivity for enlightenment, a mystical misfit named Patanjali caught a divine download. What he delivered became ***The Yoga Sutras of Patanjali***, the original open-source operating system for what it means to be alive, values-driven and on purpose. At the heart of it? The Eight Limbs of Yoga: eight simple, radical invitations to live, lead, and build from something real.

But Patanjali wasn't your average guru, as he wasn't interested in followers or fame or being the hottest item on the Vedic lecture circuit. He was more like the kind of guy who'd crash your third-eye opening, spike the chai tea with existential insight, and then disappear into a lotus field before the sun rose. Wait, don't leave! In the immortal words of that other great sage, Bill Murray in ***Caddyshack***: "There won't be any money, but when you die, on your deathbed, you will receive total consciousness." Which, let's be honest, is probably better than stock options anyway.

What Patanjali laid down was no ordinary doctrine, but instead a spinal column for the soul, built from eight shimmering limbs, each one an invitation to remember who you were before the world told you how to behave. When I went deep into my yoga teacher trainings, I started to see the Eight Limbs of Yoga not just as bendy spiritual guidelines, but as a kind of **cosmic blueprint** pointing towards contentment and fulfillment. Eight juicy steps that build on each other to help you live with more purpose, more clarity, and way less bullshit.

And here's the kicker: they don't just apply to your personal life, for they map beautifully onto how we show up in our work, our leadership, our movements.

These limbs ask you to look inward first, check your ego at the door, remember your true purpose, tune your instrument - and then guide you outward into action that's aligned, compassionate, focused, and in flow with the bigger picture. **Inner peace meets outer impact.** Namaste, but make it practical and who knows, maybe you and your business can even wake the hell up.

And no, this isn't yoga Americana as in stretchy pants and Spotify playlists, but something older, deeper and wildly more alive. The Yoga Sutras of Patanjali is a way of being.

Yoga or "union": of breath & movement; of values & behavior; of purpose & action. An inner scaffolding and eight-limbed roadmap for **turning your personal purpose into liberated leadership and the mission of many**. No, it wasn't designed for marketing plans and it certainly predates most business books by a few thousand years. However, I have found that it applies beautifully to founders who want to build something that feels awake. For entrepreneurs and intrapreneurs alike who want to feel connected to their work in the world.

So I've adapted these practices, honoring them with a grin, and a full heart, and in a way that doesn't try to mimic the sages, but to meet them in the mirror. And we begin where every cult begins: with the source. You, the original prototype, the signal center, the root frequency. If that's off, the rest is distortion and so the work starts here in the guts, in the pulse, in the reflection that doesn't flinch.

Let's walk the damn path from ME to WE to whatever-the-hell comes next. From founder with a flicker to a crew with a cause to a full-blown movement that can't help but catch fire. **We're not here to build empires. We're here to build something alive** that flutters in the gut and cracks open hearts. The kind of cult that doesn't steal your soul, but hands it back to you with better lighting.

Let's make meaning contagious.

Let's build the thing that changes you, then them, then maybe the whole damn story.

Ready?

THE
CULTIV8 CODEX

Eight codes for founders who give a damn
& desire a path to liberated leadership

"Those who are crazy enough to think they can change the world usually do."
— Steve Jobs

"Climb to the top of a ladder and then take one more step."
— Zen Koan

What you're holding is rooted in ancient wisdom and built from a scaffolding that's guided humans toward purpose, healing, and contentment for thousands of years. For me personally, this path has been essential to my evolution as a human, a father, a partner, and a leader aspiring to increase joy and reduce suffering on this rock hurtling through space and time.

I am not claiming to have invented it. I just listened, integrated what works for me, translated what I could into founder-speak for those aspiring to build a regenerative purpose-driven movement, and gave the whole thing room to breathe. There's still a little Sanskrit in the mix, but don't let that scare you off. You don't need to chant, memorize anything, or twist yourself into a pretzel. You just need to know when something true is rising beneath the noise and be willing to follow it.

These eight waypoints are here for the moments when you lose the thread. When your business starts moving faster than your clarity can keep up, or when your voice doesn't sound like your own anymore. This is a remix, offered with reverence. As stated before, the Eight Limbs obviously weren't made for startups or career pathing, but they translate surprisingly well because at the core, they're about coherence, presence, and staying true when everything around you is trying to pull you off center. Look, if something has lasted thousands of years and still vibrates with relevance, I'm paying attention.

Think of this as your inner architecture. The part no one sees but everyone feels. The rituals that shape the resonance and the true dojo inside the collective.

I call it **The Cultiv8 Codex.** It's part ancient roadmap, part founder's mirror. A set of initiations to help you tune your inner instrument until the people around you can feel it and want to play along. Each one comes with something to wrestle with, something to try, and something that might just change how you show up along your *leadership learning path*. With each code comes an opportunity to lean into an emergent leadership style through reflection and practices with the power to unlock even more potential.

We'll dive into each of them in a moment.

But first, here's the full sequence.

Leadership Learning Path	Code	Yoga Limb
Foundational Leadership	Code 1: Call Your Own Bullsh*t	yamas - Ethical Scaffolding
	1. Scale Without Scorching (ahimsa) 2. Truth or Consequences (satya) 3. Steal Less, Create More (asteya) 4. Where Your Energy Goes Your Cult Grows (brahmacharya) 5. Let Go or Be Dragged (aparigraha)	
Reflective Leadership	Code 2: Tending The Temple	niyamas - Inner Alignment
	1. The Founder Cleanse (shaucha) 2. Grateful AF (santosha) 3. Burn, Baby, Burn (tapas) 4. Know Thyself, Before You Scale Thyself (svadhyaya) 5. Faith In Flow (ishvara pranidhana)	

Leadership Learning Path	Code	Yoga Limb
Grounded Leadership	Code 3: Take Your Damn Seat	asana - Position & Posture
Regulated Leadership	Code 4: Breathe Before You Broadcast	pranayama - Life Force
Discerning Leadership	Code 5: Tune Out to Tune In	pratyahara - Signal Protection
Focused Leadership	Code 6: Fierce Focus	dharana - Single Pointed Focus
Embodied Leadership	Code 7: In The Zone	dhyana - Embodied Presence
Liberated Leadership	Code 8: Congrats, You're Fired	samadhi - Enlightened Coherence

The Cultiv8 Codex is the inner tuning fork and frequency that makes the whole damn thing hum. The path you walk here takes you from foundational to liberated leadership and the coherence built becomes the difference between a brand that buzzes and a movement that moves.

The leadership learning path shows the benefits that emerge when we simmer at medium-low heat in the secret sauce squeezed from a sacred structure old as dirt and twice as reliable: the Eight Limbs of Yoga. A path to liberated leadership. And by the time we're done, you'll have more than a business… **you'll have a living, breathing signal tower for the world to tune into.**

In the pages ahead, we'll break down each of these eight codes into actionable practices. Stuff you can walk with, wrestle with, and return to. Real tools for when the world gets messy and your mission starts to wobble.

Let's get into it.

Foundational Leadership

Every movement, every culture, every business that lasts, hits a moment where honesty either takes the wheel or gets shoved into the trunk. This code lives right there. It's where leadership stops being something you talk about and starts showing up in the small, boring, unglamorous places that quietly tell the truth. Foundational leadership doesn't announce itself. It shows up in what you tolerate, what you protect, and what you're willing to clean up when it would be easier to look away. Before anything meaningful can grow, something has to settle. Trust. The kind that builds slowly and tends to stick around.

CODE 1
CALL YOUR OWN BULLSH*T *(YAMAS)*

"Your beliefs become your thoughts, your thoughts become your words, your words become your actions, your actions become your habits, your habits become your values, your values become your destiny."

— **Mahatma Gandhi**

"The universe is watching. But mostly, so is your team."

— **Modern mystic slash strategist**

Before you build the brand, ship the product, or rally the troops… **check your damn alignment with the world around you**. The real work starts way before the launch: it starts in the mirror. In the space between what you say you value and how your business actually behaves. This is the soul scan. The gut check. Coherence between the purpose and values of the founder & the mission and actions of the company. Before you go live or go loud… go honest.

Think less brand voice and more about the places where your values are a costume. Where the stated mission is a mask and where your mouth says one thing, while your hiring process, calendar, or pricing model says another. Ethics are not window dressing; they're not about putting a list of values on a wall or reciting a vision statement in pitch decks. They are how the soul of the business reveals itself in the day to day.

Resonance doesn't happen when you're shape-shifting to please a ghost, it happens when you **lean into authenticity and stop faking clarity you haven't found**. You know that friction that you feel when something sounds good on paper but feels off in your bones? Map that.

Get curious about what you're overcompensating for and pay attention to what feels scripted. Then strip away what no longer fits. **First the revelation then the exorcism and finally the integration.** The commitment to stop pretending and a willingness to stop outsourcing your truth.

We start with the yamas: the first limb of yoga, Code 1 in the Cultiv8 Codex, and the original "golden rules" before HR got involved. While each of the eight codes stands alone, some, like this one, come with a constellation of core teachings inside. In this case, five principles that form the foundation of the whole system.

Think of them as your **ethical scaffolding** or the real stuff that governs how you move through the world, how your company shows up, and how not to be an energetic dumpster fire in your relationships, org chart, or towards the planet.

These are universal do's and don'ts. Cosmic boundaries and spiritual bumpers for your founder bowling lane. And no, you don't need to be a monk to practice them, just a human who doesn't want to build a business/cult that burns people or the planet out.

Here's the cheat sheet:

1. Do No Harm *(ahimsa)*, the call to do no harm in thought, word, or deed;

2. Truthfulness *(satya)*, the courage to speak and live in truth;

3. Non-stealing *(asteya)*, respect for time, labor, and ideas;

4. Right use of energy *(brahmacharya)*, reminds us to direct our life force toward what really matters;

5. Non-possessiveness *(aparigraha)*, the art of holding lightly and letting go.

Long before I knew the language of the yamas, I was already brushing up against their edges. I was 25, living the dream deep in the Los Angeles music scene, discovering what felt like the road to El Dorado. But eventually it became obvious that the price of admission might be becoming someone I never wanted to be.

Wanting to take a shower every time I walked out of a "successful" meeting with a label was a pretty clear indication that I was sacrificing my soul on the slab of success. I could feel when a decision, a campaign, or a client relationship didn't sit right in my body, even if it made sense on paper. I didn't always have the clarity to act on it, but over time, that internal knowing sharpened and became a compass I could lean into.

Think of the yamas as **your and your company's *soul contract* with the world**. These aren't just "best practices" or "ESG initiatives," they're the invisible handshake your brand offers to the planet and its people. Want trust, loyalty, love? Start here and call your own bullshit.

1.1 Scale Without Scorching (*ahimsa*)

Leadership gets real when growth no longer justifies damage.

"Ahimsa is not a policy of the weak. It is a weapon of the strong."

— **Mahatma Gandhi**

"Just because it's legal doesn't mean it's kind."

— **Recovering Attorney at a Conscious Business Retreat**

Do no harm: **simple words, hard practice.**

"Do no harm" isn't just for monks and medical professionals. In business, it means building something that doesn't wreck the planet, erode your team's sanity, or make people feel like crap just to sell a product. Designing a business that heals instead of harms? That's not soft or boring, it's **badass and revolutionary.**

In business, harm often wears a subtle mask. Burnout is harm, creating a culture of silence is harm, extracting more than we can replenish from people or planet, or even ourselves, is harm. Guru, our agency, was founded on the mission we carry forward today: to increase joy and reduce suffering by catalyzing business solutions to humanity's greatest challenges of climate action, mental health and healing food systems. It was all about the what, but for the first few years we were in existence I forgot about the how and continued to grind big agency expats in the name of purpose-driven progress.

Ahimsa calls us into a culture of care. A place where the drive for impact doesn't eclipse the humanity of those delivering it and where we measure success not just by what we build, but by how we build it. It begs the question, how can you deliver your product or service in the most conscious way possible, to scale without scorching?

Reflection:

Where does harm still live in our systems, either through exhaustion, exclusion, or erasure? Where are we pretending "it's fine" when it's clearly not fine? Where are we trading long-term healing for short-term hustle? Run your company through this ESG (truth serum) lens:

E is for Environment

Planet: What's being quietly torched in the name of speed or scale? What's getting extracted, dumped, flown, or "offset" so we can launch on time? Is your supply chain full of words like "eco" and "sustainable" but built on hope and greenwashing?

....

....

....

S is for Social

People: Who's winning and who's paying the invisible price? Think labor. Think customers. Think communities downstream from your brilliance. Is anyone getting exploited, ghosted, underpaid, or "burned out, but still grateful"? (Yes, this includes your interns.)

....

....

....

G is for Governance

Power: Are decisions made with care, clarity, and accountability, or are you still texting your team at midnight and calling it leadership? Who gets a voice? Who gets left out? Does your culture match your values, or just your merch?

....

....

....

Practice: The Ahimsa Audit
(AKA Are we Accidentally Being A-Holes?)

This is your chance to pause the hustle, zoom out, and look at the real ripple effects - not just what you make, but how you make it.

Step 1: Trace the Path

Break your product/service delivery down into 3–5 key stages and list them. Think of this as your business's life cycle. For example:

- Ideation / Design

- Sourcing / Production

- Team Operations

- Marketing / Messaging

- Delivery / Post-Sale

Step 2: Scan for Harm

For each stage, answer this:

- Who or what gets depleted here?

- Where is there friction, burnout, or collateral damage?

- What part of the planet or people pays the hidden cost?

Don't justify. Just write.

Step 3: Find the Small Shift

Big systems take time. But every revolution starts with a small repair and yes, ***small flowers can crack concrete***. Pick one thing on your list that you could:

- eliminate (because it's just legacy harm)
- redesign (so it's not extractive)
- acknowledge (because silence is harm, too)

Write it as a commitment:
We're shifting __________ by __________ because __________.

Optional Bonus: Build the Altar

Place that commitment somewhere visible, on your team chat, in your studio, on your fridge. The altar is a reminder that your values aren't just beliefs. They're behaviors.

1.2 Truth or Consequences *(satya)*

Foundational leadership starts when the truth doesn't need a spokesperson.

"The truth will set you free… but first it will piss off your board of directors."

— **The one investor who actually meditates**

"If you don't lie, you don't have to remember anything."

— **Mark Twain**

Let's be honest, and I mean actually honest. Truthfulness in business isn't about radical transparency for its own sake. It's about not gaslighting your audience, your team or even yourself. Because here's the deal: **Authenticity beats perfection every single time.**

People can sniff out spin like a bloodhound on espresso. If your brand is selling sunshine while your product burns down rainforests, guess what? They're gonna find out. And then they're gonna post about it. Loudly. **This is not the era of perfect brands, but the era of human brands that are messy, clear, self-aware, and just vulnerable enough to admit they're still figuring it out.** As a dear friend of mine once said, "vulnerability is sexy."

Too many founders treat branding like a dating app: swipe right on their best angle, airbrush out the weird stuff, and hope no one asks about the time they accidentally "laid off" the wrong person. But real connection that builds cult-like followings, mostly happens through truth. And truth doesn't mean oversharing or emotional dumping, but alignment between what you say, what you do, and how you show up when nobody's watching.

Another company I founded, Maha Global, works with Fortune 500 companies to evolve their reputation intelligence and has found that it isn't those that simply have the best reputation that win, but those that have the smallest delta between what they say and what they do. Or said another way, the gap between stakeholder's sentiment in specific areas vs the company's behavior in those same areas. Purpose washing just ain't gonna fly anymore. Be accountable. And for that matter, "purpose-hushing" ain't gonna fly either. Be proud.

Share the journey, not just the destination. For example, just because you won't be net zero for another decade doesn't mean you shouldn't be proud of where you are and where you're going. So say it before they do: " We're proud of this, but we're still working on that," "we're learning," "we're listening," "we're growing." It's amazing how disruptive a little honesty can be, especially in a world full of misinformation and disinformation. Truth can build trust. **And trust is the currency that makes cults possible.**

Reflection:

What's one uncomfortable truth your company needs to start telling your team, your customers, or yourself? The one truth your team knows but no one names, because it makes things awkward? And what would shift if you said it unapologetically, as an invitation to grow,?

Practice: Satya Sweatlodge

Step 1: Name the Truth You're Avoiding

Write down the sentence your comms team would rather bury. Use these prompts:

- "The truth we haven't been saying is…"

- "What our team knows but our customers don't is…"

- "If we were fully honest, we'd admit…"

Step 2: Map the Risk (and the Opportunity)

Get clear about what you're afraid of and what might open up. Fill in the blanks:

If we told the truth about ____________, we're afraid people would ____________.

But if we did it well, people might actually feel ______________________________.

Step 3: Craft Three "Truth Posts"

Try three flavors of honesty. You don't need to publish all three, you're testing your tone.

1. The Proud and Imperfect Post

"We're proud of _______. We're working on ______. Thanks for walking with us."

2. The Mirror Moment Post

"Here's what we said. Here's what we did. Here's what we learned."

3. The Invitation Post

"This is where we're stuck. This is what we're exploring. This is where we need your input."

Step 4: Choose One and Ship It

Pick the one that makes you slightly sweat and share it (on social media, a newsletter, your site, or internal team chat). If it's not a little scary, it's not satya.

Bonus Round: Truth Integration

Schedule a "Satya Session" once a quarter with your team. Ask:

- What are the truths we're not saying out loud?
- Where are we posturing instead of practicing?
- What truth could set us (and our brand) free?

1.3 Steal less, create more (*asteya*)

Foundational leaders don't treat other people's time and energy like free refills.

"You might not rob banks, but you do steal time, credit, and calm. Daily."

— **A burned-out Executive Assistant**

"You can have anything you want, but not everything you want."

— **Peter Drucker (Top Management Consultant)**

Asteya, or "non-stealing" is the art of not taking what isn't yours, even when capitalism says "everybody else is doing it". The misguided quote "Good artists copy, great artists steal" is often attributed to Pablo Picasso, but being a "great artist," he may very well have stolen it from someone else and used it to his own benefit.

In business, theft isn't just about pirated logos and unpaid interns. No one's stuffing laptops into backpacks here. We're talking about the quiet, everyday theft that hides in your calendar, your email, your unconscious sense of entitlement to other people's energy. It's the meeting that should've been a message and the intern whose brilliance gets folded into your "thought leadership." The cultural wisdom you borrowed without remembering where it came from. It's often subtle, socially sanctioned, and hiding behind your Q2 roadmap. Stealing shows up as:

- **Lifting ideas without credit**
- **Wasting your team's time like it's free tap water**
- **Over-promising with no intent to deliver**
- **Marketing that plays on people's insecurities just to sell them back their self-worth**
- **Squeezing vendors, margins, or junior staff so the founders can fly business class to Burning Man**

At the agency, we often run these strategic "Puhpowee playshops" that integrate exercises to get various stakeholders to think differently about their business. Over the years I've aggregated many of these practices to get leaders to play on purpose and recently upon review of what some of our strategists had in their latest and greatest hits I found that we may not be giving full credit to where they came from. We've now confirmed a complete citing of sources and catalyzed a culture of gratitude for the genesis of great work that we utilize for the benefit of our clients. The truth will set you free, hallelujah!

In short: **just because you're not robbing a bank doesn't mean you're clean.** Most stealing happens in the name of fear…fear that there won't be enough…enough attention, enough innovation, enough market share, enough time to be "first." It's actually a scarcity reflex, but let's be real: What if instead of hoarding, mimicking, or rushing, you built from abundance? That's when originality actually shows up, generosity is baked in and your work regenerates energy instead of just extracting it.

Integrity doesn't end at the boundary of your own mind, but extends outward into how you handle power, recognition, and reciprocity. It's a call to come back into right relationship with time, ideas and the people who make your magic possible and recognizing that if you're building a cult worth joining, it better not be built on invisible labor and spiritual shoplifting.

Because in a world built on taking, creating without stealing is quietly revolutionary. And businesses that give more than they grab are the ones people follow, fund, and tattoo on their forearms.

Reflection:

Where in your company are you taking more than you're giving? What are the changes you might make with more of an abundance mindset? What would shift if your brand became a net giver of joy, trust, energy, credit, and/or time?

....

....

....

....

....

....

Practice: The Integrity Inventory

Ready to feel a little called out? Good. Take a moment to audit your business across these dimensions:

• **Time Theft:** Are you wasting people's time with meetings that could've been emails… or emails that could've been nothing?

• **Idea Theft:** Are you crediting the people who inspired, sparked, or built this work? Or are you "repurposing" a little too hard?

• **Energy Theft:** Are you asking more from your team than you're willing to model? Burning them out while praising "tenacity"?

• **Emotional Theft:** Are you marketing with manipulation? Using shame or urgency to sell solutions that don't match people's real needs?

• **Planetary Theft:** Are you consuming more than you replenish? Is your supply chain full of good vibes, or just good margins?

1.4 Where Your Energy Goes Your Cult Grows *(brahmacharya)*

Attention is the first place foundational leadership either tightens or leaks.

*"Attention is the altar. Don't worship bullsh*t."*

— **Modern Founder Proverb**

"The difference between successful people and really successful people is that really successful people say no to almost everything."

— **Warren Buffett**

Let's talk about energy. That current that runs through your bones when you're focused, when your work clicks, when you know that you're leading with something that actually matters. I'm not talking about vibes, or your startup's sustainability report, or the deck that says "We value hustle" while half your team quietly plots their exit. I mean your life force and the actual voltage it takes to think clearly, build something true, and stay upright while doing it.

It's about knowing you only have so many good decisions in you each day before you start spiraling into project management purgatory or signing on to things your soul didn't co-sign. You burn through your clarity chasing vanity metrics and wind up with a polished brand and a body that twitches every time your phone buzzes. There was a time when "grinding it out" and "crushing it" was considered a business plan, but that time has passed and hustle…well, it's not a strategy. We are done with glamorizing burnout and calling it grit.

This isn't about renouncing pleasure or buying robes and disappearing into the forest with a bowl and meditation bell. Brahmacharya in business means **using your energy and other's like it's sacred, because it is**. It's asking: Does this task feed the mission or just feed the algorithm? Am I running toward purpose… or just sprinting in a hamster wheel made of KPIs? What if we worked from coherence instead of exhaustion? Where is your sacred yes getting diluted by a thousand half-hearted maybes?

In founder-land, energy leaks faster than funding rounds. You burn the candle at both ends and then wonder why everything starts smelling like smoke. **Sacred focus** means remembering that your presence is the most valuable currency in the room. It means not offering up your nervous system to the gods of the attention economy before breakfast. It means knowing when to say no, not because you're unavailable, **but because your yes is holy.**

Don't just think of this as time management. It's about energetic fidelity, holding a line with your attention, and recognizing that every distraction, every performative hustle, every dopamine-fueled detour comes at a cost, and the bill always shows up in burnout, resentment, or mediocrity. I've paid that bill more than once. Like the time I poured months into a block-chain-demystifying panda NFT, backed the "next big" social network that (turns out) nobody needed, or helped a spiritual teacher workshop their presidential campaign platform. They were shiny. They were seductive. But they scattered my signal and reminded me that just because something feels exciting doesn't mean it's aligned. Oh the medicine and the poison in what some have labeled ADHD.

true story, great story, won't put in print

Some of the biggest energy leaks are much more subtle: the "quick inbox check" that becomes 47 browser tabs and a mild existential crisis, the weekly meeting that exists only because it's always existed, and the projects that sound sexy but don't serve the core. **Here's a wild idea: just stop.** Close the tab. Kill the meeting. Drop the shiny maybe. **Focus is magnetic**. When you use your energy wisely, people feel it, lean in and want to build with you. Tired founders build tired movements, but tuned founders build businesses that hum with power and flow.

Where your energy goes, your cult grows.

Reflection:

What are the yes's you've made recently where there was not a full body yes? Where is your energy going that your soul never signed off on, and what would shift if you treated focus as a devotional act?

....

....

....

....

....

....

....

....

....

....

....

....

Practice: The Energy Audit

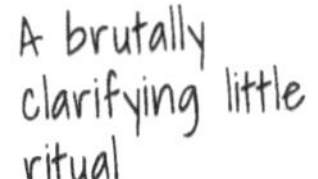

1. **List the top 3 activities** that light you up, move
    the mission forward, and actually make a difference.

1. **List the top 3 activities** that drain your soul,
    waste your time, or make you fantasize about mov-
    ing to a cabin in the woods.

1. **Double down on the first list.** Trim, delegate, or
    straight-up delete the second.

1.5 Let go or be dragged (aparigraha)

The foundation gets stronger when leaders stop clinging to what already ran its course.

"You can't receive with clenched fists."

-Possibly Rumi, possibly your head of ops

"Let come what comes, let go what goes. See what remains."

— Ramana Maharshi

In business, the art of letting go means unhooking from the illusion that your worth is tied to performance or your bank account. When we start to confuse our work with our worth, we start clinging, and clinging leads to stagnation, codependency, and eventually marketing emails that smell like desperation. **Let go**. You can't pivot if you're dragging the carcass of last year's "vision" behind you. There is power in knowing when to kill the deck, sunset the product, bless and release the client who makes your whole team tense up like synchronized swimmers if no one told them what the routine was.

We hold on, often way past the point of usefulness: to outdated metrics, to old titles, to "maybe someday" ideas, and to the belief that we have to keep pushing just because we already pushed this far. But here's the truth:

Freedom isn't found in the hustle. It's found in the release.

This is about surrendering to what is. Not in resignation, but in rebellion. It's the holy f*ck-it that happens when you realize control was never the point. You don't build something alive by strangling it into submission, but by knowing when to loosen your grip, exhale, and make space for what actually wants to grow.

People sometimes equate non-attachment with apathy, but in this case, non-attachment is what keeps the whole thing agile and breathing. It's the difference between building something that can grow or strangling it with yesterday's ideas. When you loosen your grip, the work gets smarter, products shift when they need to, teams adapt without drama and the vision evolves without losing its soul. If you can sometimes allow yourself to let go of the version you thought it had to be, you make room for the upgrade and something better gets a chance to arrive. That's when your business stops being a brand and starts becoming a force!

Let me level with you. My biggest block to releasing attachment into real liberation hasn't been sex, drugs, or even spiritual bypassing in the form of excessive journaling. It's been money. Specifically, my attachment to it. It's the sneaky boss I never hired, whispering sweet nothings like "just a little more" or "when you hit that number, then you can breathe." I've ridden the full rollercoaster: scarcity shame, cash windfalls, mission creep for big checks, and watching my spirit sneak out the back door while my ego signed new contracts. Even on a silent meditation retreat, as I was supposed to be merging with the void, my mind was planning this exact book you're holding…(along with the funding model, TED Talk strategy, and merch line.)

My spiritual teacher Ram Dass said, "You can't get out of a jail you don't know you're in." And money? It built my jail out of gold-plated purpose and equity stake fantasies.

Aparigraha, non-attachment, doesn't mean you don't care. It means you care from a different seat. You show up, you trust, you serve, you build, but you stop worshipping the financials and you don't grow for growth's sake. You start trusting the flow, not just forecasting it. Because if you're clinging, you're not creating. And if your fists are full of control, there's no room left for grace. Let go or be dragged.

If you're feeling a little more exposed than inspired right now, good. That usually means something important landed. Foundational leadership doesn't feel heroic, it feels sobering in the best way for it is realizing you can't unsee certain things anymore. This is the kind of leadership that earns trust quietly, over time, without asking for it or putting it on a billboard. It's what lets a team breathe and a culture stop bracing for impact. Nothing flashy happened here. No one rang a bell. But the ground just got steadier. And from here on out, things either get more honest… or you'll feel it when they don't.

Reflections:
The Great Unclenching

What's the project, partnership, persona, or product you're still clinging to even though it's already expired?

____

____

____

Preference is natural, but attachment is suffering. What ambitions are you attached to?

____

____

____

What is your current relationship to money and how does that impact your beliefs about "success" or "growth"? What early experiences have driven that relationship with money? How is that keeping you stuck in a loop you've already outgrown?

____

____

____

Practice: The Funeral For What No Longer Serves

Write a eulogy for what you're letting go.
Be real. Be specific. Honor it.

Fill in the blanks:

We are gathered here today to lay to rest: _______________________

____

It was born from ____

____

It served us by ____

____

But now, it's costing us ____

____

And keeping us from ____

____

Now read it out loud (yes, out loud). If you get emotional, good.

That means you're doing it right.

Now that you've stopped actively lighting things on fire, we turn inwards. This code is about reflective leadership, which means you start noticing your own patterns before they run the show. Not judging them or fixing them immediately, but just actually seeing what's there. Reflective leadership is what happens when you pause long enough to catch yourself in the act...of reacting... of rushing...of telling yourself you'll deal with that later. This is where leadership gets quieter, weirder, and surprisingly more effective. Once you see your patterns, they lose their authority, and leadership becomes steadier by default.

CODE 2
TENDING THE TEMPLE (NIYAMAS)

"Before you change the world, clean your inner desk drawer."

— **Your nervous system, probably**

"The hardest thing in the world is to simplify your life. It's so easy to make it complex."

— **Yvon Chouinard (Founder of Patagonia)**

You made it through the wild terrain of the yamas. Our not-so-gentle reminder that business is not exempt from ethics, boundaries, or basic human decency. We covered harm, truth, theft, energy, and attachment. Not in theory, but in action: going deep inside your culture, your calendar, your supply chain, and your strategy.

But now we pivot, because once you've stopped doing the things that drain your business of soul… it's time to start doing the things that charge it up. This next stretch is less about the outer guardrails and more about the inner electricity. It's where we move from restraint to rhythm, reaction to presence and compliance to coherence.

Before you can start to craft a strategy, you first need to get a clear signal. **If you want to scale authenticity, you have to be anchored in it.** This is where the work gets quieter, and more demanding.

You stop taking your cues from the feed, the funding round, or the pressure to perform and start listening from the inside out. It's the time to sit in your own signal long enough to feel its pulse. Before you plan, produce, perform purpose or pitch…pause. *ahhhhhh-literation*

Every cult begins with a founder who's willing to listen deeply enough to find his or her own authentic voice.

This is the beginning of what the old texts called niyamas, but what we'll simply call **the inner practices.** And just like every great cult has its core rituals, your business will need more than values. It will need vitality.

The shift at this stage doesn't arrive with fanfare. It's quieter than that, more like a tilt of the compass. Up until now, you've been identifying what needs to go: habits, stories, structures and illusions that no longer serve. What happens next is the slow, intentional work of shaping what manifests through you instead. It reopens a formative window, softening the clay of your being so something healthier can take form. The Niyamas offer internal scaffolding rather than external strategies or leadership hacks. These are daily disciplines that result as subtle shifts in attention that, over time, build something strong at the root.

Healthy businesses, the kind that move mountains, *or at least people* don't appear out of nowhere. They're built by leaders who know how to tend their own inner grounds. The Niyamas are that groundwork and the invisible landscaping behind cultures that vibe, systems that don't grind people down, and founders who still have a soul by the end of quarter.

Because what really shapes a company isn't just what's said in the boardroom, but lives in the spaces between words. How does trust travel through your team? Does Sunday night bring dread? Do Wednesdays feel like quicksand? HR posters can't fake this.

Culture starts in the founder's mirror.

If company culture had a trail crew clearing the path, these niyamas would be the first five with their boots in the dirt:

1. **Purity (shaucha):** Clean your space, your energy, and your intentions. Chaos is not a business model.

2. **Contentment (santosha):** Be grateful for what is, not just hungry for what's next.

3. **Discipline (tapas):** Do the work, especially when it's unsexy. Sweat can be sacred.

4. **Self-Study (svadhyaya):** Know your patterns before they run your company.

5. **Surrender (ishvara pranidhana):** You're not the source, you're the signal. Let it through.

These are orientation points and important reminders of how to stay close to what matters when the noise picks up and your calendar starts to colonize your nervous system. You don't need to get them right, that's not the point. The point is to stay in relationship with them, to keep showing up even when it's messy, and to let the practice reshape you slowly, from the inside out - tending the temple.

2.1 The Founder Cleanse (shaucha)

Reflection sharpens when the signal isn't buried under everything else.

"Clutter is nothing more than postponed decisions."
— **Barbara Hemphill (Leadership Consultant)**

"When the mind is pure, joy follows like a shadow that never leaves."
— **Buddha**

Let's be honest: purity sounds a little... uptight, but in business, purity isn't about bleach wipes and matching brand decks, it's about **clarity.**

Clear space → Clear mind → Clear signal.

Because chaos, clutter, and old baggage don't just live in your storage closet. They live in your calendar, your KPIs, your decision fatigue, and your vaguely panicked team meetings. Before realizing the importance of this, I was weighed down by a six figure inbox constantly beckoning for me to play email racquetball. And every time you try to build something beautiful on top of a pile of digital and emotional debris, you end up with a shiny new product... running on old stale bandwidth. Shaucha invites us to clear out what clouds our field: toxic habits, cluttered values, and misaligned partnerships; to help us cultivate clean inputs, clean language and clean intention.

Nothing kills momentum like confusion and nothing speeds things up like clarity. When your workspace is a mess, your brand story's a jumble, and your vision deck is now 137 slides of incoherent aspiration, then your team can't move. Clutter doesn't just sit there. **It's a tax on energy.**

I didn't see the cost until I cleaned house. What I once wore as a resilient, tenacious badge of honor was quietly suffocating me. Clearing it all created space to breathe, think, and lead. Control what you can and breathe through the rest. Preferably without a clogged N95 mask.

Purity in business means:

- Tidying your systems

- Cleaning your language

- Clearing the noise from your mission

We're not aiming for perfection here, just making sure people feel that they can actually breathe, build, and belong. Because clean doesn't mean sterile, it means ready. And when you cleanse your space, mind, and mission, then the magic has somewhere to land.

Reflection:

Do a full energetic audit of your company: What feels murky? What needs to be composted or cleared? Where in your business are you tolerating low-grade chaos? What would become possible if you treated clarity like a strategic asset instead of a weekend project?

....

....

....

....

....

....

....

....

....

....

....

....

Practice: The Founder Cleanse

Pick one zone of your business to purify today. Just one.
Then attack it like a monk with a label maker. Options:

- **Your desk:** Yes, including the weird snack wrappers and six unread copies of Fortune Magazine.

- **Your inbox:** Archive, delete, or - radical idea - just unsubscribe.

- **Your mission statement:** Read it out loud. If it sounds like it came from a brand AI bot, rewrite it until you feel something.

- **Your meeting calendar:** Cancel what can be an email. Or a nap.

Then pause.

Notice the energy shift that comes with the cleanse?

That's signal returning.

2.2 Grateful AF
(santosha)

A reflective leader can enjoy the view without immediately redesigning it.

"He who is not contented with what he has would not be contented with what he would like to have."

— **Socrates**

"You are perfect just as you are, and you could use a little improvement."

— **Shunryu Suzuki**

Let's talk about **satisfaction**. And I don't mean the one that comes with a six-figure ARR spike or a surprise exit. Somewhere along the way, contentment got misfiled under complacency, like it was something to grow out of once the real ambition kicked in. As if peace and progress were incompatible. As if resting in what's good would somehow dull the edge of what's next.

In a culture addicted to striving, santosha asks something different and reminds us that wholeness isn't waiting on your next win. It's right here, in the unfinished. In the fact that you've made something real enough to stand inside. It's the pause where breath returns and joy has a shot at slipping through the cracks. It's that rare moment when the chase lets go of your collar and you get a glimpse of what's already working, **because hard work without contentment is just frantic tap dancing in a broken elevator.**

Taking time to lean into gratitude doesn't mean that you're lowering the bar. It just gives your nervous system a bit of help to catch up to your progress. Once you recognize that what you've built is not a final destination to get to, you will realize that it is something already worthy of celebration.

Celebrating early traction on an underfunded creative campaign with a young, inexperienced team punching well above our weight back in the early years of guru was one of the most satisfying days of my career.

Celebrate where you are. Celebrate every small win. Celebrate the fact that you're building something that doesn't suck the soul out of everyone who touches it. And if you're not there yet? Celebrate the fact that you know it. That you care. That you're in motion. Be grateful, beyond the guilt, because contentment doesn't mean settling it means seeing. Because when you build from satisfaction instead of scarcity, people feel it and a founder who can **be here now by being grateful AF**, can truly be a magnetic signal in a world addicted to the next best thing.

Reflection:

Where have you been too busy striving to notice what's already thriving? What part of your business quietly brings you joy and how could you honor that more? What might change if contentment became your foundation instead of your fallback?

....

....

....

....

....

....

....

....

....

Practice: Gratitude for What's Working

List three things in your business you're genuinely grateful for today. Not the marketing gloss. The real stuff: A team member who makes things better just by being in the room, a client or customer who gets it, or a process that no longer makes you want to scream into a pillow. Name it. Feel it. Don't rush it. Then share it with someone.

Let your gratitude compound.

Witnessing gratitude being shared is proven to carry with it exponential benefits. Give someone that opportunity.

2.3 Burn, Baby, Burn
(tapas)

Discipline is what keeps reflection from evaporating.

"Through discipline comes freedom."
— **Aristotle**

"Devotion starts where dopamine drops off."
— **Start Your Own Damn Cult, marginalia edition**

Let's talk about **tapas**, and no, not the kind you share over sangria while avoiding the real conversation. This is the fire, the burn, the long-haul stamina, the one-foot-in-front-of-the-other-even-when-it-sucks kind of energy. Discipline in business isn't about spreadsheets and Gantt charts, it's about devotion. It's what you return to when the dopamine fades and the metrics aren't flattering. It's also the thing that keeps your mission alive when all the "fun" parts are over and the strategy slide deck is now your emotional support animal. The shamanic aphorism rings true, "everyone wants to do the ayahuasca but nobody wants to do the dishes."

There's a special kind of energy that shows up when you do the thing you've been avoiding: the email, the money convo, the hard feedback, the solo work that requires more presence than pizzazz. It's the sacred sweat, that heat, and the friction that forges. It's not punishment, it's purification and it's about devotion. Tapas is the business equivalent of sitting for your mediation practice even when the sun is shining and the waves are pumping. Said another way: to stick with consistent practice aimed at a deeper vision even when the shiny shortcuts show up.

In my world of marketing some of the world's most impactful brands and movements, discipline often looks like running certain processes for what seems like the thousandth time, because if we trust the process the work gets better.

For instance, even when my inner oracle is convinced our big idea is a winner (it sounded undeniable in the echo chamber of our own enthusiasm) **we still test and learn.** So even when we know this campaign has legs, we still test it and put our cleverest copy and creative work through the gauntlet of real human feedback. We're no longer just idea factories, we're customer whisperers. We ground our gut instincts in data, not just vibes. This is where creativity meets science, where fire meets framework. Discipline means trusting the process… even when I'm impatient, even when I'm busy, even when my ego wants to skip straight to the billboard reveal. Because that's how we build work that doesn't just flash, it lands and engages. The work is proven through a process that is proven. Discipline and devotion to our highest potential.

Daily discipline, on the other hand, is about consistent commitment - something that, over time, becomes muscle memory. It's a cornerstone of steadiness, especially when things get chaotic. Two core practices that have carried me through both the highs and the lows? **1)** sitting in meditation for at least fifteen minutes a day; and **2)** taking a breath before I speak, especially when I'm triggered.

Sounds simple. It's not.

As the old Zen saying goes: "You should sit for 20 minutes a day. Unless you're too busy, then you should sit for an hour."

Tapas isn't about proving something, but about realizing that nothing burns brighter than a purpose that's been refined by fire. **Discipline, when done right, is not oppressive, it's clarifying.** It turns chaos into cadence and that has the potential to turn your business into something trustworthy for you, your team and your future to count on.

Most people don't burn out because they're doing too much, they burn out because they're doing too much of the wrong thing, too far from their own center. Are you still connected to the purpose behind the effort? Tapas, in its truest sense, invites you back into alignment through consistent chiropractic adjustments and reminders of why you started in the first place. The right type of fire will refine and recalibrate.

Burn, baby, burn.

Reflection:

Where do you show up only when it's sexy or visible, and what would it look like to commit quietly, daily, any way? What kind of founder would you become if you built from consistency instead of adrenaline? What are some ongoing disciplined practices that you could bring into your work on a daily basis?

....
....
....
....
....
....
....
....
....
....
....
....
....
....
....
....
....
....
....

Practice:
Do the One Thing You've Been Avoiding

Do the one thing you've been avoiding right now, not later. Pick the task, convo, or commitment that keeps slipping to the bottom of your list. The one you secretly hope will disappear on its own. Now do it with intention. Then celebrate like you just raised a round without pitching anyone. Rinse repeat same day same time every week.

2.4 Know Thyself, Before You Scale Thyself *(svadhyaya)*

Reflective leaders study their own patterns before asking anyone else to change.

"Study thyself, discover the divine."

— **Patanjali**

"If you can't lead yourself with clarity, please stop trying to lead a team."

— **Everyone's inner employee**

"Polish The Mirror"

— **Ram Dass**

This is the art of self-study or, in business terms: the practice of becoming the **kind of leader people actually want to follow**. Self-awareness isn't just a nice-to-have. It's a leadership prerequisite. It's also the original anti-burnout strategy, the key to emotional intelligence, and the first internal filter before any meaningful launch or commitment.

and not just because you're the one who approves payroll

You can read all the business books, attend every founder retreat in Tulum, and microdose your way through your entire Series A…but if you're not looking at how your unconscious conditioning is shaping your decision, you're just building a bigger maze for yourself to get lost in. If you don't know how your own patterns play out under pressure? You're simply scaling dysfunction. Faster.

Self-study is essentially about understanding your internal operating system. Where do you hide when things get hard? Where do you overcompensate? Where do you spin, soothe, or sabotage your own clarity? And most importantly: Where is your shadow leading without your consent?

Do try this at home, but not in isolation, because self-awareness gets sharper in community. This doesn't require a business fortune teller or spiritual guru. Just an honest coach, a co-founder, or a radically transparent friend who won't let you get away with your default scripts. Welcome those that compassionately wield the sword of truth. Make space for feedback that's not about performance but about unconscious patterning and then don't just receive it. Reflect on it, give gratitude for it, journal it and **practice not practicing it.** 

For me, the realization came in the form of an inspiring, impactful mission powered by a burnt out team. My constant visioning, chasing and then expectation to execute at all costs was fraying the central nervous system of our agency. And because I don't like letting anyone down, especially changemakers coming to us with incredible world elevating initiatives that needed our brains and services to be birthed into the world, I was letting my team down by never saying no.

When you know yourself, you don't just lead better, you build better. You stop reacting and instead start responding and becoming the kind of founder others don't just work for but who they want to grow with. And that kind of leadership? That's how movements start.

Reflection:

What story do you keep telling that no longer fits who you're becoming? Where are you leading from fear or habit, rather than clarity and presence?

....

....

....

....

....

....

....

....

....

....

....

....

Practice: The Blind Spotter's Guide

What's one blind spot you have, but haven't named? Maybe it's defensiveness in meetings, avoiding conflict, people pleasing or leading with urgency instead of clarity. Name it. Stare it down. Write about it for 5 minutes. Then share it with someone you trust and ask for accountability that doesn't come with shame. Then ask that person to name your actual blindspots, because the definition of a blindspot is that you don't see it… meaning that what you named is most likely a self referential superpower at best or a shameless plug at worst.

Practice: Who The Hell Are You

Self indulgent? Yup. Little awkward? Yup. Psychedelics? Bonus. This code is about becoming acquainted with the person you think you are. Here is an exercise that will help you do that: Find a mirror and spend twenty minutes in a deep eye gaze with yourself. Follow Ramana Maharshi's meditation of self inquiry by repeating the question: "Who am I?" If speaking out loud, make sure to close the door or you may end up in a psych ward.

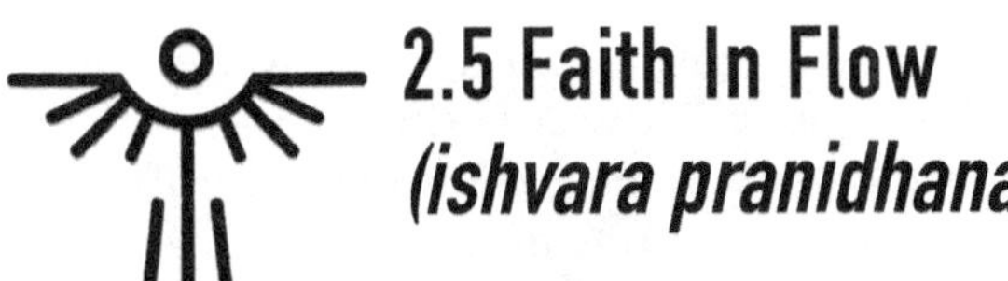

2.5 Faith In Flow
(ishvara pranidhana)

Reflection sometimes looks like getting out of the way.

"Do your work, then step back. The only path to serenity."
— **Lao Tzu**

"Surrender isn't giving up, it's getting out of your own damn way."
— **Overheard in a Founder therapy retreat**

Founders are trained to grip, to forecast, to own every outcome and to white-knuckle their way through uncertainty like they're personally responsible for the tides, the trends, and the algorithm. Somewhere along the line, leadership got tangled up with the idea of control, as if holding tighter was the same thing as leading better. But control has a cost, and more often than not, the currency is your clarity...and your team's sanity.

Real leadership isn't about control. **Control is just a beautiful illusion with a really high burn rate.** What if it was about collaboration with the unknown? Surrender to something greater, trust, and take the ultimate exhale that signals you're ready to stop micromanaging the universe.

Ahh, the illusion of the all-knowing founder. The thing is that you're not omniscient or omnipotent. You're a complicated kaleidoscope of skin, sweat, intention, and dirty chai trying to do something meaningful with limited data. Your job is to build something adaptable, not to play God. As Buckminster Fuller said, "the universe is synergetic." Do your best, build the systems, show up and then hand it over to something bigger; to your team, your clients, your community, the intelligence of the ecosystem and culture you helped shape but can't fully predict. The truth is that **if your business can't breathe without you gripping the wheel, it's not a business...it's a hostage situation.**

The pandemic hit like a cosmic curveball, and while most agencies were trimming headcount like it was Black Friday at HR, we did something wildly impractical: we kept the whole damn crew. No mass layoffs, no panic-pivot, just a quiet commitment to ride the rapids with integrity. We figured if we were going to get tossed around, we might as well do it together…helmets on, hearts open. And it turns out, that decision didn't just preserve jobs, it forged something rare. We came out of the storm with a crew that was more bonded than ever, scarred maybe, but scarred together. And ready. Not just for business as usual, but for business as it could be.

You make plans and still steer, but with the humility to know you're not laying the road brick by brick. You trust the rhythm of timing, the wisdom in letting go, and the possibility that something more intelligent than your timeline might be waiting to unfold.

In that space, the one between action and allowance, a different kind of leadership emerges. When you have faith in flow, you evolve into shared leadership that knows when to step back so something wiser can come forward.

If this code felt quieter, don't mistake that for softness. This is where leaders start catching themselves mid-pattern, mid-story, mid-eye-roll. Reflective leadership makes you harder to surprise with your own behavior. You begin to notice the old moves before they fully play out. Sometimes you pause. Sometimes you laugh. Sometimes you do the same thing anyway, but with your eyes open. From here on, leadership gets less reactive and more intentional. Not saintly. Just awake enough to choose.

Reflection:

Where are you pretending to have control and what is that costing you? What part of your business feels tight, clenched, or "held hostage" by your own expectations? Where can you release without retreating?

Practice: Hand It Over

Pick one decision you're gripping too tightly: the rebrand, the launch, the hire, the next funding call. Now, for two full minutes, breathe and imagine handing it over: to the universe, to the deeper intelligence of your team, to the mystery that knows more than your OKRs ever will.

What wants to happen here, if you stop forcing it?

Listen.

. . . .

Grounded Leadership

At some point, leadership stops being about insight and starts being about presence. You can feel it when someone walks into a room and things settle instead of speed up. This code is about grounded leadership, which has less to do with what you know and more to do with how you arrive. Grounded leaders don't need to convince anyone they're in charge. Their posture and gravitas do the talking. This is where leadership drops below the neck and starts to hold its weight.

CODE 3
TAKE YOUR DAMN SEAT (ASANA)

"People don't follow ideas. They follow energy."

— **Founder folklore, passed down over overpriced coffee**

"The most powerful tool you have is your own example."

—**John Wooden (Legendary Basketball Coach)**

Let's get one thing straight: in yoga, asana isn't just about a strong downward dog or physical practice. Asana, in its original form, simply means "a steady and comfortable seat." The posture you take when you're ready to show up with presence. So here's the question to ask yourself honestly: in your business, **have you taken your seat?** The deeper energetic seat that's built on groundedness, holds steady during conflict and doesn't flinch when the spotlight hits.

Leadership is a posture, not a position. This code asks: How do you show up? In meetings? In hard conversations? On stage, on virtual meetings, or at the Tuesday team check-in? Are you rushing, performing, posturing, pushing? Are you grounded enough to lead without bulldozing, and clear enough to speak without spiraling? Real? Human?

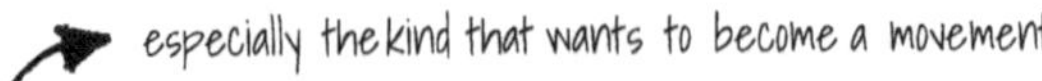

Because in business, **presence is everything.** It settles the nervous system of the team, clarifies what matters, and creates the kind of empathetic space that makes honest collaboration possible. When you're really in your seat, you're not chasing the next big thing, because you're too busy anchoring the current one. In a world wired for speed, your centeredness slows the field. It creates safety, clarifies chaos and says: "We're good. Let's breathe. Now, let's build."

Your company's energy mirrors your own. If you're scattered, it'll be chaotic, but if you're centered, it'll resonate. And people don't trust brands that feel fake, **they trust brands that feel *embodied*.** You don't need to convince, you just need to be where you are and let that presence speak.

That's what Asana looks like in a business:

- Embodied leadership

- Clarity in tone

- Grounded messaging

- Marketing that feels less like manipulation and more like magnetic truth

This is where the energetic shift from Me to We begins and the movement starts to take shape. When you're centered, others don't need to guess who they're following. They know. And from that knowing comes trust. From that trust, momentum.

Since day one, Guru had a clear mission: increase joy and reduce suffering. Noble. True. But if I'm being honest, for a long time it felt like a serious mission. The kind that made you sit up straight and use your board room voice. And while I believed deeply in the "what," the projects, the impact, the change, I never quite felt at home in the "how". Seriousness never fit me right. I've always been more at ease with rascals. Teachers like Ram Dass, Tom Robbins, Roshi Joan Halifax, Dave Chappelle…the ones who smuggle wisdom in through the side door. The ones who laugh as they teach, and teach as they laugh.

When spiritual teachings migrated from East to West, we dressed them up in earnestness. And the same thing happened with impact work. Nonprofits and social enterprises alike, all suited up in solemnity. As if meaning couldn't be met with mischief. As if the how always had to mirror the what.

spirituality
is serious
damnit

I fidgeted under that weight, just like I fidgeted in my seat as a kid. For the first few years of Guru, I kept adjusting my posture, trying to look the part of the serious CEO. But it wasn't until I gave myself permission to bring my full self — the playful, pun-loving, trickster energy — into the work that I finally felt like I'd taken my true seat. Not just a seat. My seat.

Now I can look my team, my clients, the world in the eye and say with a grin:

Let's play on purpose.

Every founder needs to define their stance. Too many confuse positioning with persona, adopting language and posture that mimic someone else's success or try to overly differentiate from the competition rather than clarifying their own truth. When you sit in a role that doesn't fit, you leak energy, but when you claim the seat that's actually yours, everything around you begins to align.

More than a brand position, it's the gravitational center of your business. It shapes the tone you speak in, the choices you make, and the way your community responds. And when that steady seat is real, rather than reactive, people feel it, lean in and stop scanning for red flags.

Rather than being bold or unique for the sake of it, stay true to what you actually stand for, even when the market shifts and even when it feels exciting to pivot into something shinier. If you don't claim your position, someone else will fill in the blanks, and what they write probably won't do you justice.

So take your damn seat. Take it like it matters and let it shape your leadership, your culture, and your impact. Let it be the place you come back to and build from, again and again. Positioning isn't performance. Again, it's devotion.

If this code did its job, you're not thinking much about leadership right now. You're here, in your body, with a sense of gravity that doesn't need commentary. Grounded leadership doesn't rush to respond or scramble to prove it's in control. It moves at the pace of what's actually happening. When things wobble, it stays long enough for the noise to settle on its own, which is often all that's needed. You don't have to announce this kind of leadership. People feel it, and more often than not, they steady themselves in response.

Reflection:

If no one else was watching, what would your business still stand for? Where have you been trying to sound right, instead of being real?

....

....

....

....

....

Practices:
Leadership as a Full Contact Sport

- **Pause before you speak.** Let your body and brain arrive before your words do.

- **Walk meetings.** Movement invites insight. Shift the context, shift the conversation. (At Guru, we give out prizes to whomever does the most walk meetings in a week.)

- **Check your seat.** Literally. Are your feet on the floor? Are your shoulders in your ears? Are you breathing?

- **Name the energy.** If tension is in the room or in the business, don't override it. Surface it with care. We call this playful exercise, "the stinky fish"…where everyone says the thing, because the longer you walk around with the thing the stinkier it gets.

- **Set rituals that reconnect you to your body.** Even a one-minute grounding practice before meetings can recalibrate the whole field.

- **What's one embodied cue you can anchor into to lead from a deeper place?** (For example: relaxing your jaw before speaking, taking one conscious breath before replying, placing both feet on the ground during online meetings, or scanning your body for tension before decision-making.)

- **Positioning rewrite.**

    1. Take your current brand positioning statement, pitch deck, or about page.

    2. Cross out every sentence that feels borrowed, bloated, or bullshit.

    3. Write a new paragraph not to sell, but to speak from your seat.

    4. Ask: If this were my last day to say what I believe, would this be it?

Once you're grounded enough to stay, the next step is how to move. Regulated leadership lives in that small, crucial space between stimulus and response, right before the old reflexes make their pitch. Not rushed or bracing for impact. Just available. Breath shows up here as a quiet partner, less a technique and more a truth-teller. Leaders who can regulate themselves don't just make better decisions. They change the tempo of the room. And when the tempo shifts, everyone is invited in to play.

CODE 4
BREATHE BEFORE YOU BROADCAST *(PRANAYAMA)*

"Exhale, you're not defusing a bomb. You're sending an email."
— **Startup Sutra, Verse 4.0.2**

"The mind is the king of the senses, but the breath is the king of the mind."
— **B.K.S. Iyengar**

"Breathe properly, stay curious, and eat your beets."
— **Tom Robbins**

This is the practice of breath, rhythm, and energy management that determines whether your leadership lands as a calm transmission or a panic attack. If the pace of your business and your body are out of sync you're not building a movement, you're building a migraine. Breath is infrastructure, ignore it, and the whole damn system gets twitchy. If you're holding your breath during launches, check-ins, or client calls - something's off. If your team can't exhale, your culture is a pressure chamber, not a playground.

Everyone talks about time management, but energy management is the real flex and breath is the metronome. **Breath is a business practice**!

Returning to the breath is my go-to reset button, and honestly, I hit it a lot. Like, hundreds of times a day. Whenever my mind spins out or my body tightens up like it's prepping for battle, **I pause. I breathe. Three deep ones. That's it. Just enough to shift the channel from panic to presence.**

It sounds simple, and it is, but it's also profound. This tiny act rewires your nervous system in real time. You're literally switching from fight-or-flight mode sympathetic nervous system (SNS) to rest-and-digest mode parasympathetic nervous system (PSNS). SNS for survival, performance, speed and getting shit done to PSNS for recovery, connection, creativity, listening and long-term health. From "oh shit" to "I'm good." No meditation cushion required. **Just breathe. It's the original reboot: always available, totally free and wildly underrated.**

Just like breath regulates the body, the way you move energy through your business regulates the nervous system of the whole company. Every company breathes but some wheeze, some hold, some hyperventilate. And if you're fried, scattered, or slowly bleeding out under a smile that says "I'm fine," it probably has less to do with your calendar and more to do with your breath. Or lack of it. Let's look at it a different way: Just like breath calms the nervous system, clears the fog, and brings the body back into alignment, it can do the same for your business. It can steady the chaos, sharpen the signal, and remind the whole system what it's actually here to do.

Inhale ➞ Internal Alignment

This is the sacred pull inward. The deep, unglamorous inhalation where you stop pitching and start paying attention. You turn down the noise. You tune in. You remember why you started this whole circus in the first place.

This is the breath that happens before anything looks good on a whiteboard. It's where the founder drops the persona and listens to the signal underneath all the noise. If you try to build from the exhale without ever taking this breath, you'll end up launching beautifully branded bullshit that no one remembers.

Hold ➞ Relational Coherence

Here's the pause. The place where the inhale settles into stillness, and your vision either coagulates into cult magic or collapses under the weight of your ego.

This is where your team, your investors, your community start to feel it… whatever "it" is. If the inhale was real, the hold becomes magnetic. You're not broadcasting. You're resonating. It's a shared hum that doesn't need a slide deck to explain itself.

This is also the phase where most founders freak out and try to fill the silence. Don't. Trust the pause.

The hold is where the room syncs up and your **stakeholders align into a flow state.**

Exhale ⟶ External Amplification

The release. The broadcast. The let-it-fly.

Here's where the thing you've built finally starts moving on its own. If the breath before it was clean, the exhale doesn't need to hustle. It lands, reverberates and starts showing up in other people's language, in their invitations, in the quiet moments when they say, "There's something about this that feels...different." Amplification isn't about shouting louder. It's about having something that breathes true enough to carry on the wind.

If your nervous system is shot, your business will mirror it. If your breath is shallow, your team will run on panic. But if you learn to pace your inhale, respect the hold, and trust the exhale, something bigger than you will start to breathe through it all. This isn't just breathwork, it's founder hygiene. And yeah, it might be the most sacred **KPI** you'll never put in a pitch.

Yes, there is a wellness trend of breathwork. That's not what this is. When you breathe, you interrupt urgency, reclaim clarity and tell your nervous system: I got this. From there you speak more clearly and you lead more intentionally. In a nutshell, you make less stupid decisions, because breath is the backchannel to your best leadership. Energy precedes action and if we want our leadership to be regenerative, our nervous systems have to be too.

This is where Me to We gets visceral, because breath doesn't just regulate you, it co-regulates your team. If you breathe like a cornered animal, guess what? Everyone else gets dysregulated too. But when you breathe...you create rhythm...and rhythm creates flow...and flow is what your team's been begging for in all those clunky "internal culture" meetings. Breath creates coherence and coherence is what makes a group of people feel like a cult instead of a calendar invite.

Business can be breathwork to a beat. And if you lose the rhythm, sure, you'll still be moving, but it'll be all gas, no groove. You'll burn out your team, garble your message, and forget why you started in the first place. So before you hit send, go viral, or launch that next big thing? Pause. Inhale what matters. Exhale the noise. Then speak like someone who's actually listened. **Breathe. Then broadcast.**

If this code landed, you may notice a little more space showing up before you respond. Nothing dramatic. Just enough room to choose differently than you might have before. Regulated leadership lives in that space. It doesn't promise perfect timing or flawless composure, but it does make it harder for every trigger to take the wheel. Over time, that small shift adds up. Conversations soften, decisions clarify, and the room starts moving at a pace you can actually work with. You didn't manage any of that. You just learned how to breathe before you move.

Reflection:

Where in your business are you holding your breath, literally or energetically? What decisions or dynamics are compressing your rhythm? How might your leadership shift if you let breath set the tempo?

....
....
....
....
....
....
....
....
....

Practice: The Business Breathalyzer

- **Breathe, then decide.**

  - Sit still, feel your breath, inhale clarity, exhale urgency.

  - Ask: "What do I know in my gut? What does my breath say? What's the signal beneath the noise?" Write it down. Then decide.

- **Sync with natural rhythms.** Align strategic work with peak energy times. Don't force deep visioning at 4pm.

- **Exhale culture.** Celebrate pauses. Model pacing. Give people permission to recover.

- **Watch the energy drain.** Notice the meetings, relationships, or habits that leave you chronically depleted.

- **Use breath to reset momentum.** When stuck, shift your physiology before shifting your plan.

  - Close your eyes. Inhale for 4. Hold for 4. Exhale for 4.

  - Ask: Does this pace match the way I want to lead?

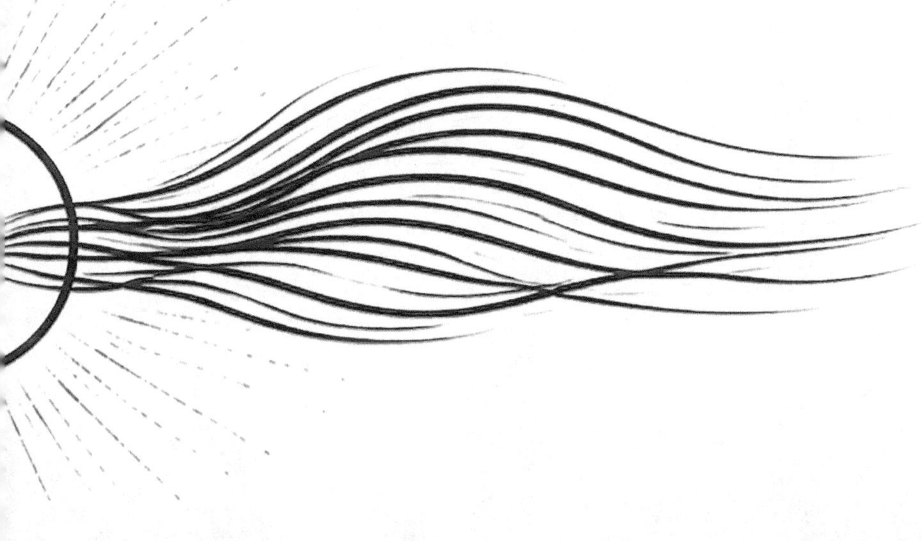

Discerning Leadership

Now comes the part most leaders skip because it messes with their habits. It begins when you decide who or what you will make yourself available to. Not everything deserves. Not everything deserves your attention, your reaction, or your energy, no matter how urgent it pretends to be. Pratyahara is the practice of tuning out the noise on purpose, not to disappear from the world, but enough to hear something more accurate underneath it. Discerning leaders don't withdraw because they're overwhelmed, they with-

CODE 5
TUNE OUT TO TUNE IN (PRATYAHARA)

"The quieter you get, the more you can hear."
— **Ram Dass**

"Unplugging isn't a luxury. It's survival."
— **Scribbled on a retreat center bathroom wall**

"The times are urgent; let us slow down."
— **Dr Bayo Akomolafe**

Welcome to the lost art of tuning in by tuning the noise out. If your nervous system has ever needed a safe word, it's probably because you've been stuck in…well….the world today. Media bombardment, inbox chirping, newsfeed baiting, board deck, project management ping, another strategy call about the strategy call. You know the drill, you've seen this movie before and you realize that you don't have to react to everything.

Focus isn't built by white-knuckling harder. It's built by dialing down the interference.

encouraged even

You are allowed to disconnect, decouple, and yes, occasionally go full digital detox, so you can reconnect to the signal that actually matters: **your own.**

You can't lead if you can't hear yourself think and you sure as hell can't build a movement if you're dancing to every distraction that barks at you. This is where discernment meets design. Leadership requires sensory boundaries and if your business only survives when you're endlessly plugged in, it's not a business, it's a treadmill with branding.

Here's a plot twist for all you founder-influencers: *You don't need to be "on" all the time.* You need to be on point. Your team doesn't need more updates, they need you to be able to sit in silence long enough to hear the difference between urgency and truth. The greatest cults in history were led by people who understood the power of retreat. Silence isn't a break from leadership. It's part of the job description.

the good kind, and the weirdly successful kind

At Guru, we've leaned into the idea of a regenerative business that encourages people via a four day work week to go get into the woods, spend time with their families or at least take a break from meeting mania to tune into their own signal and find their flow. **Decolonize the mind, regenerate the soul, and rewild business** by pushing back against the accepted modern myths of business as usual.

Many businesses are either obsessed with the competition, chasing culture, or lost in so much noise they miss their own signal entirely. So they repeat what's trending, regurgitate what sells, and end up building something that sounds fine and feels hollow. Silence is where the sharp stuff lives. Not the emptiness, but the edge. It's where you hear what no one else is brave enough to wait for: the better way, the stronger narrative, the truer offer, the signal beneath the static.

When you remove the excess input, the signal strengthens. You stop broadcasting noise and you start broadcasting resonance. And in that rare golden moment people don't just hear you, they feel you.

Tune out. Tune in. Cultivate signal.

If this code landed, you may notice a strange new freedom showing up. Not the freedom to do more, but the freedom to ignore things without explaining yourself. Discerning leadership isn't loud or reactive. It's calm enough to let most of the noise pass by unanswered. When you stop feeding every signal that demands your attention, something steadier takes over. Your focus sharpens. Your decisions simplify. The world doesn't get quieter, but you do. And from that place, it becomes much easier to tell what actually matters.

Reflection:

What noise have you normalized that actually disconnects you from your own vision? Where is distraction stealing your clarity? What would your leadership feel like if silence wasn't empty, but strategic? What feels loud, but unimportant?

....
....
....
....
....
....
....
....

Practices:
The Alt+Control+Delete Protocol

- **Digital fasts.** Two minutes a morning, one hour a day, one day a week, or one weekend a quarter devoted to non-doing without screens. Let the system settle.

- **Clarity days.** Block a full day each month for quiet thinking, big-picture visioning, or integration.

- **Sensory audit.** What inputs are flooding your field? How do news, noise, and notifications shape your mood or mindset? What feels loud but unimportant?

- **External silence, internal listening.** Step away from feedback loops. Ask yourself: What's my perspective? What signal is actually coming from me?

- **Nature as recalibration.** Go to the ocean, the trees, the sky. Somewhere you can remember true scale and perspective.

- **F*ck Your Phone.** Turn your off phone and wait at least an hour. Before turning it back on, close your eyes, put your phone on your lap, and turn it back on. Notice what you feel as the notifications bombard your central nervous system. Reflect.

the
more
the
merrier

Once you've reclaimed your attention, the question changes again. Not what's possible, but what actually matters. This code is about focused leadership, which has very little to do with productivity hacks and a lot to do with courage. Focus means choosing one direction and letting the rest stay unfinished, unanswered, or slightly disappointed. It's the moment leadership stops orbiting everything and commits to something. Focused leaders don't try to do it all. They decide, and then they stay with the decision long enough for it to mean something.

CODE 6
FIERCE FOCUS (DHARANA)

"I don't have ADD, I just... what was I saying?"

"Multitasking is the art of screwing up several things at once."
— **Steve Uzzell (National Geographic Photographer)**

Come on in and stop multitasking like a glitchy octopus, welcome to the code of one-pointed attention, also known as the ability to focus on something for longer than the lifespan of a social media reel. You've got tabs open in your browser, your brain, and your soul and you're definitely not alone. Oh ADHD, the thousand island dressing in so many startup salads, and certainly a key ingredient in my own unique brand of movement building. Like many attributes that make a strong charismatic visionary leader, it comes with medicine and poison. I've managed my own with a mix of daily mindfulness and periodic psychedelic retreats. actually we call them entrepedelic retreats (email me).

Modern leadership often looks like a never-ending tap dance between strategy, crisis, innovation, and "just circling back on this." And your attention is being slowly auctioned off to the highest notification. So today, try this:

Pick one thing. Hold the thread. Ignore the circus.

Cut through the noise and point your energy like a laser instead of a strobe light. The signal sharpens and people know you mean it. The focus is felt. The founder who can say "no" 90 times This is how people know you mean it. The founder who can say "no" ninety times to protect one potent "yes" builds coherence that's contagious and focus becomes a form of power. You will be tempted. Good ideas will flirt with you, dressed in urgency and FOMO, looking all shiny and sounding all strategic. Stay in the pocket, stay in the zone.

Focus isn't forceful: it's faithful. It's the quiet discipline of returning again and again, until effort gives way to flow and progress begins to compound. When attention is sustained, work organizes itself around clarity. Momentum builds. Congruence follows. And the thing you're building finally receives your full presence and what you're working on finally has enough of you to come alive.

The truth is that every great cult and every movement that endures has a core obsession, a reason to exist, a gravitational center. Something you keep returning to, even when everything else begs for attention. Dharana teaches this kind of loyalty.

It's not about tuning in once and hoping for the best, but about staying with the thread long enough for something meaningful to take root. **You don't need more ideas, you need fewer escape routes.** Protect the core, design systems that keep it nourished and respect the guardrails that keep you from veering off into performative noise. Because when you build around what actually matters, that focus doesn't just hold your business together, it gives it form. It gives it a spine and people feel it. When your message sharpens, culture follows. Focus fiercely.

*If this code did its job, you may notice a drop-off. Not in ambition, but in bullsh*t. Less second-guessing. Less orbiting the edges. Code 5 helped you stop feeding the noise. This one shows you what happens when your attention finally chooses a home.*

Focused leadership brings a quieter confidence where you're no longer managing distraction; you're honoring direction. Over time, that choice simplifies how you prioritize and how you show up. The work starts to feel less scattered and more intentional, not because the world got clearer, but because you did. And from that place, what you're building carries a different weight. It holds. It lasts.

Reflection:

What would meaningfully advance your mission if it received sustained, uninterrupted focus? What deserves your best energy, but is currently getting your leftovers? Are you protecting deep work like a sacred ritual? Where are you confusing motion with progress?

This practice helps leaders distinguish between activity and impact.

....

....

....

....

....

....

....

....

....

....

....

....

....

....

....

Practice: The Attention Audit

Each week, name the one big thing that moves the needle on your mission. Just one. Then block time for it, protect it like it's your weirdest, best-kept cult secret and tell your team so it becomes real. Let everything else serve that one thing - or wait.

Practice: The Distraction Audit

Each week track everything that breaks your focus from that one big thing that moves the needle on your mission. What's essential? What's ego? What's habit? Most importantly, what is your strategy to let go of each distraction? Now go Marie Kondo on your workflow.

From Lisa Arie's
StillPoint Experience

Practices to Deal With
The Attention Economy

- **Sacred scheduling.** Block time on your calendar for deep work and treat it as uninterruptible. Don't push it off. Protect the container.

- **One goal, one window.** Keep one tab open. Choose one intention for the session. Let it breathe.

- **Start with stillness.** Begin focused work with a breath, a bell, a ritual. Give your mind a place to land.

- **The art of saying no.** Every yes to distraction is a no to your deeper work. Refine your filter.

- **Completion over compulsion.** Resist jumping to the next thing. Let closure be a form of clarity.

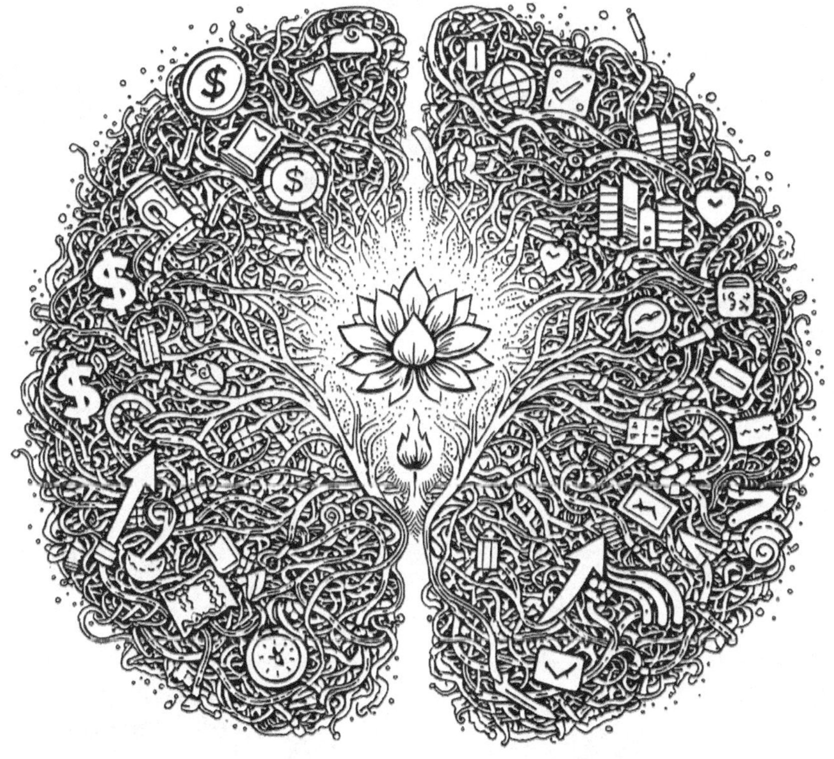

Somewhere along the way, the work stops feeling like something you were managing and started feeling like something you were living. This code is about embodied leadership, which shows up when the practices you've been leaning on quietly become the way you move through the world. There's less effort here and fewer reminders. You don't have to think about staying focused or regulated because your behavior already knows what to do. Embodied leadership has a kind of ease to it, not because things are simple, but because you're no longer fighting yourself while doing them.

CODE 7
IN THE ZONE (DHYANA)

"In flow, every action, movement, and thought follows inevitably from the previous one, like playing jazz."
— **Mihaly Csikszentmihalyi (Father of Flow)**

"There are only two mantras, yum and yuck. Mine is yum".
— **Tom Robbins**

When your energy, attention, and purpose are in sync, you stop forcing and start transmitting. Dhyana isn't about sitting cross-legged on a mountaintop trying to silence your thoughts. It's about staying so tuned in that the signal drowns out the static.

This is the code of absorption. When you remember that **you're not a human doing, but a human being.** This is when you're no longer "working on" your business, it's working through you. Time blurs, doubt quiets, and what's left is rhythm, resonance, and the sacred hum of harmony. Pulsing with the current rather than pushing the plan.

Be Here Now ⟶ Here Now Be ⟶ Now Be Here

You're inside the thing you built and it's breathing you. The kind of presence that doesn't flinch, split or scroll. In the zone, where flow takes over. Devotion moves into motion and ultimately into absorption; both individually and collectively. Coherently. Contagiously. Mindfully cultivate the contagion.

If you're preaching balance, but emailing your team at midnight - it leaks.

If you claim to stand for joy, but your culture feels like a pressure cooker - it shows.

If you market depth, but make decisions from fear - your signal fractures.

This is the check-in point: Are you living what you're selling? Or just narrating the aspiration? This is where the cult either deepens or breaks, because people don't follow charisma forever, they follow coherence and a founder whose daily presence says: "This is what we do. This is who we are. This is how we be."

An embodied leader who finds this flow, quickly becomes contagious and lights up the family, friends, team and community around them both intentionally and unintentionally.

Flow is far from woo woo, it's actually neurological. It's also the birthplace of your best ideas, your weirdest metaphors, and your most alive business decisions. The zone is real and you can build it, because flow is a trainable state, but not with burnout Olympics or post-its…with presence.

We often mistake flow for luck, or luxury…like it only happens on a powder day or during your morning dance party with the kids. Flow doesn't need perfect silence or a mountaintop; it just needs alignment. It's the natural rhythm that emerges when everything clicks into place.

Here's how we do it at Guru: when someone joins the crew, I ask them two things —

1. If you had to work on one mission for the rest of your life, what would it be?

2. What gets you into flow?

Then we design from there. We match missions. We honor rituals. Not because it looks good in a company values deck, but because it works. People who are lit up from within make luminous things. Ideas, campaigns and businesses start to move like jazz with clear intention and improvisational genius. Nothing is quite as rewarding for a proud purpose-driven biz Papa or Mama as when their team settles into an aligned flow.

This doesn't mean you've "made it," but it does mean that perhaps you've graduated to a version of leadership that truly radiates and aligns. The mission lives in your body, your leadership and your team now." Then fine to end with bigger text that is there.

Welcome home. Welcome to the zone. Stay a while.

If this code lands, you may notice something mildly inconvenient: people are now paying attention to what you do, not what you say. Embodied leadership has that effect. It shows up in the small, repeatable moments, the ones you don't think to curate. Leadership has moved into your habits now. Which means it's working. And it means you're living it, whether you're on your best behavior or not.

Reflection:

Where are you asking others to buy into something you haven't fully claimed for yourself? What would shift if you moved from speaking about your values to living them more visibly? What could your company become if flow was the standard, not the outlier?

....
....
....
....
....
....
....
....
....
....
....
....
....
....

Cult Practice: Find Your Flow

Ask yourself: What conditions help you drop in? What environments, times of day, or rituals invite your clearest attention? What kills it instantly (hint: team chat, email, meetings titled "alignment")?

Now: Schedule a 90-minute block to be in it. No interruptions. No performance. Protect it like it's a portal, because it is.

Cult Practice: Design for Flow
(Team Edition)

What helps your team get into collective flow? Do they know what flow feels like, not just what it looks like? Flow scales when it's shared. Build the conditions for your people to lose track of time... in the best way.

- **Quiet check-ins.** Begin meetings with one minute of silence or mindful breathing. Let presence set the tone.

- **Non-reactive listening.** When tension arises, don't rush to solve. Stay with the energy and let clarity arise naturally.

- **Notice your impulse to fill.** Silence is often where the real wisdom waits.

- **Collective genius.** Make space for every voice. There's brilliance hiding in the quiet corners, creativity tucked inside unexpected places. Diversity of experience isn't just beautiful, it's a generative force. Listen wider.

From Lori Hanau's GRTL CoHere Journey

Liberated Leadership

By the time you get here, leadership isn't something you're chasing or trying to get right. It's just happening. This code is about liberated leadership, which tends to show up when you stop gripping the whole thing so tightly. You still care. You still act. You just aren't hauling your identity, your résumé, and your inner critic into every moment. You do it all with a little more play, a little more trust, and a lot less tension around how it all turns out. What's left is leadership with a bit more room in it. And oddly enough, things work better that way.

CODE 8
CONGRATS, YOU'RE FIRED (SAMADHI)

"Enlightenment is when a wave realizes it's the ocean."

— **Thich Nhat Hanh**

"Your work is to discover your work and then with all your heart to give yourself to it."

— **Buddha**

This isn't just absorption. This is transmission.

You've done the outer and inner alignment, the breathwork, the truth-telling, the ritualized disciplines, cleared the nervous system, tuned your signal, and embodied the message. These weren't just tools, they were portals and now, something else is taking over. Call it the current, the culture, the field…it doesn't matter. What matters is **you're not running the show anymore. The signal is.**

This is it, the exhale after the exhale. Samadhi, in business terms, is when leadership becomes unnecessary as a performance. The culture holds the signal without supervision. The work moves correctly without charisma, urgency, or enforcement. You haven't just embodied the values, you've distributed them. What remains is not control, but trust.

The founder becomes optional, not irrelevant, but non-essential to day-to-day coherence. That's the graduation point most leaders never reach.Far from viral success, this is collective coherence. The tension is gone, the work has its own rhythm and it's moving through you like music. Your team starts speaking in harmony, not just alignment. The work moves like jazz…unrehearsed, but undeniably in tune.

For us, at Guru, the confirmation came from clients overheard saying, "This is what we've been waiting for," while their customers started parroting the message before the brand team even finished the campaign. It's like the whole ecosystem caught the same signal at once and now everyone's nodding, reposting, quoting, and pretending they saw it coming. That's when you know: you've gone from alignment… to transmission. This is not something forced, but you can *cultivate* the conditions for it. And when it lands? Damn.

You're not the founder gripping the wheel anymore, you're the one keeping the channel clear. The work is breathing the team now. And from this tiny flower that cracked concrete, ripples flow outwards amplified for anyone tuned to the right frequency to hear. People can feel it and they want in.

I've had glimpses and been let into the room just long enough to taste the sweetness, but humbly offer that samadhi remains a code where I currently ride shotgun joyfully on the journey with my fellow travelers rather than reaching any sort of dreamy destination.

This is the moment your personal frequency becomes a shared field.

Not leading with effort ⟶ *leading from liberation.*

If this code lands, you may notice yourself taking the work seriously without taking yourself quite so seriously. Liberated leadership looks like showing up fully, then letting go of how it's received. You still lead. You just don't need to hold it all together anymore. Nothing here needs to be clung to, not the practices, not the titles, not even this book. Take what's useful. Leave the rest. Go live your life. Leadership will meet you there. This is Liberated Leadership and this is where the cult catches fire.

Reflection:

What would it look like to trust that the thing you've built is already bigger than you and your role now is to keep the signal clean, the culture coherent, and the current moving?

Where is your team already holding the signal and how can you support it without taking it?

If your leadership dissolved into legacy today... what would the work carry forward without you at the helm?

Liberated Leadership Practice: Let It Be Enough

This isn't a meditation to improve anything. There's nothing to fix, optimize, or transcend here.

Find a seat and let your body settle.

Notice that this moment is already happening without your permission. No effort required.

You don't need to agree with them, but see what loosens when you gently offer yourself the following reflections:

I am not in control of everything that happens.

You can stop pretending now. It's a relief.

The roles I play will change or fall away.

Leader. Founder. Fixer. The one who knows what's going on.

You're allowed to put them down occasionally.

The work will continue with or without me.

This is not an insult. It's good news.

What I offer matters, and it is not all that I am.

Let contribution and identity stop sharing the same chair.

I don't have to hold it all together to belong here.

Notice what softens when effort eases.

Now sit with this question for a moment, without trying to answer it:

Who am I when I stop trying to be someone?

If nothing shows up, perfect. That's kind of the point.

Before you move on, notice something ordinary: the weight of your body, a sound nearby, the fact that the world is still turning.

Then stand up and return to your day.

Not enlightened. Not finished. Just a little less tightly wound.

Purpose Isn't a Vibe, It's a Practice

- **Revisit your why.** Purpose fades without repetition. Regularly return to the question: Why does this work matter to you, really?

- **Work from resonance.** Say yes to conversations, people and projects that light up your nervous system, not just your calendar.

- **Protect your genius.** Guard your creative flow like it's IP. Spend more time in the parts of your work that feel like expression, not obligation.

- **Design for devotion.** Build systems that serve your soul, not just your schedule. Let your values shape your velocity.

- **Let it be enough.** Sometimes alignment is quiet. Don't mistake peace for stagnation.

OUTRO: FROM FOUNDER TO FOLLOWER

"Our greatest human adventure is the evolution of consciousness. We are in this life to enlarge the soul, liberate the spirit, and light up the brain."

— **Tom Robbins**

"You are the sky. Everything else is just the weather."

— **Pema Chödrön**

Maybe you picked this book up looking for a formula. Some tidy methodology to help explore that 2 a.m. gut feeling that your business isn't just a business. That it is trying to become something else. Something truer, riskier, more alive. Maybe you were trying to bring coherence to the chaos. Maybe you were trying to figure out what to build or where to join in the first place. Maybe you were just trying to remember how to give a damn without losing your edge.

Whatever brought you here, you stayed, you read, you scribbled in the margins. You walked through each of the eight codes, even though some of them might have been mirrors you didn't quite want to look into. You tuned your instrument. You took your seat. You let go. You started listening to the parts of yourself that don't talk in bullet points.

And now - here you are. A little clearer. A little more cracked open. Possibly allergic to your own marketing language. That's good.

Nobody tells you that when you do this work right, when you build something with this much honesty, **the result doesn't look like mastery**. It looks like mystery. The thing you've built stops orbiting around you and starts developing a rhythm of its own. And your role shifts. You're no longer the center of the story. You're part of the system. You're the one listening to what the cult wants next. You begin to see that the sharpest strategy is often silence, and that the most trusted founders are the ones who've learned how to follow what they helped bring through.

You stop proving and start tending. You let the business become its own kind of intelligence, shaped by your hands, absolutely, but not owned by them. It grows past you, surprises you and if you're really paying attention, it humbles you. The business remembers why it exists, what it came here to do and actually does it.

Because the work isn't about being the loudest. It's about staying in tune and harmonizing with the ecosystem around you. To notice the shift when momentum becomes movement. When the team stops looking to you for all the answers. When the culture starts self-correcting. When the soul of what you've built shows up in places you never expected it to.

This is not the part where you take a bow. This isn't a victory lap. No finish line where you emerge enlightened and invoice-ready. There's just the work. The showing up. The tuning in. The steady devotion to something that might always be a little too wild to fit in your five-year plan. You throw another log on the fire. You hold the door open for the wind to catch the spark.

The journey from founder to follower isn't a downgrade. It's the destination. It's what happens when you build something real enough to transcend you. When you stop gripping and start offering. When the business breathes without being micromanaged. When the team moves in rhythm without being puppeteered.

Shared Leadership for your team ⟶ Liberated leadership for you

This manifests when the clarity, values, and responsibility you once carried alone are metabolized by the whole. Decision-making spreads. Authority becomes contextual, not positional. People step forward because they feel the work asking, not because they're waiting for permission. This is the moment a cult matures into a culture and a founder becomes a follower of the thing they helped set in motion. When leadership is truly distributed, the work doesn't weaken without you at the center, it gets stronger. That's the measure of success. Not how many people depend on you, but how many no longer need to.

So let it keep getting stranger, truer, more alive. Keep going. All blessings on your beautiful, bewildering, batsh*t crazy journey.

Keep the fire lit. Lead less and listen more.

The cult is calling.

About The Author

A Jewish businessman, a Buddhist yogi, and a Hindu lover walk into a bar. Setup for a joke?

Nope, just the strange cosmic cocktail that is Gagan Jared Levy.

Jew-Bu-Du, spiritual strategist, creative instigator, and cultural mycologist who's been quietly helping build the most alive movements of the past two decades - socially responsible business, impact investing, regenerative agriculture, psychedelic healing, and even pitched in on a little campaign called Obama '08.

As former Co-Chair of the Social Venture Network (the folks who helped birth B Corp), he's helped redesign capitalism with a conscience. As a board member of Ram Dass' Love Serve Remember Foundation, he's worked to carry ancient wisdom into modern hands without watering it down. A visionary bridge between the business and spiritual worlds.

He founded guru, an award-winning creative agency that helps CULTS (Conscious Undeniable Love-filled Truths) take root in business, brands, and culture. His most recent initiative is guru's creative playground and innovation lab, Puhpowee, through which this book and other exciting, visionary projects sprout and infect culture from the fertile soil of creative minds.

He's also the co-founder of Maha Global, an AI-powered platform that leverages brand reputation and stakeholder sentiment to hold Fortune 500 corporations to a higher standard, because good intentions don't change the world if they're not backed by behavior. He is also proud to sit on the boards of the impactful hunger relief organization Conscious Alliance and PACT (Psychedelic Arts And Culture Trust). And has fun rousing and inspiring students as a sporadic adjunct professor at his alma mater University of Colorado's advertising school.

Whether on stage, in ceremony, or scribbling strategy on the back of a napkin, Gagan helps leaders build with soul and scale with integrity. His mission is to increase joy, reduce suffering, and remind business what it's capable of when it remembers its true reason to exist. When it remembers its purpose.

This book is part of that remembering. 

Share your cult starting and scaling success & stay in touch: connect@WeAreGuru.com

PuhPoWee

"Puh-pow-ee" originates from the Anishinaabe language and translates to: "the force that causes mushrooms to push through the earth overnight" or the "unseen energy that animates life."

Puhpowee is an innovation lab within Guru's culture centered design ecosystem.

Really, we're **cultural mycologists that rewild business and regenerate culture** by designing strategies rooted in nature's intelligence and cultural alchemy.

Ideas, like mushrooms, wildly sprout from the fertile soil of creative minds – bringing forth a kaleidoscope of imagination. They burst with vibrant hues and unique shapes, intertwining and dancing to form new perspectives. Like hungry foragers, we eagerly pluck these ideas, nurturing and shaping them into creations that ignite inspiration and good – breathing life into the world around us.

Beneath it all, strategy moves like the unseen mycelium -- subtle, intelligent, and deeply connected. It feeds the creative ecosystem, steering the wild emergence of ideas toward coherence, relevance, and regenerative impact. What appears spontaneous is rooted in intention.

What grows wild is guided by design.

GAGAN J LEVY
Founder of Guru, Puhpowee, Maha Global
& Your humble sherpa on this adventure

weareguru.com
gotppw.com
maha.global

Gratitude

Marguerite Hofmeyr - This book wouldn't have gotten the breath of life it needed without you. Your love, partnership and wisdom have lifted me into a more expansive version of myself than I knew was possible. (sentiency.co)

Ram Dass - Sitting at your feet, absorbing your wisdom and love has been a blessing for me and my family. Thank you for reminding us to keep our hearts open. (RamDass.org)

Raghu Markus - Your friendship and mentorship have been a steady blessing in my life. Thank you for leaving footprints—and occasionally a good laugh—for me to follow. (beherenownetwork.com)

Lori Hanau - Your coaching and friendship have shaped me into a better leader and a better human. Thank you for teaching me that shared leadership actually works. (grtl.us)

Christy Brown - Learning the true meaning of yoga through your training was monumental in shaping both me and this framework. Thank you for grounding the work in real practice. (christybrownyoga.com)

Baha Fenerci - Thank you for the creative partnership and for always bringing beauty, depth, and a sense of play into our work. (driftroot.com)

Jocelyn Kay Lee Levy - Learning with each other over the past two decades has made me a better man and a better father. Thank you for your support, for the deep yoga training and for the co-parenting journey we continue to walk together. (weeyogis.com)

Mom and Dad - I wish every child the love, joy, and confidence you infused into my life. Thank you. I love you.

To every business partner, colleague and mentor I've had the privilege to work with - thank you for walking the path with me.

Art by: DriftrootArt Co.

Notes

Notes

Notes

Notes

Notes

Notes

Notes

Notes

Notes

Notes

Notes

www.ingramcontent.com/pod-product-compliance
Lightning Source LLC
Chambersburg PA
CBHW022013170726
47994CB00026B/3179